ENGLISH
LAKE
COUNTRY

1 Swaledale sheep

DUDLEY HOYS

ENGLISH
LAKE
COUNTRY

LONDON

B. T. BATSFORD LTD

First published 1969
© Dudley Hoys 1969

Text printed in Great Britain by
Northumberland Press Ltd, Gateshead, Co. Durham
Plates printed and books bound by
Richard Clay (The Chaucer Press) Ltd, Bungay, Suffolk
for the publishers B. T. Batsford Ltd,
4 Fitzhardinge Street,
London W1

7134 0064 1

CONTENTS

ILLUSTRATIONS

The illustrations listed above are reproduced by kind permission of the following: Noel Habgood, 1, 2, 5, 11, 13, 17, 22, 23, 24, 27, 29; Edwin Smith, 3; Kenneth Scowen, 4, 9, 10, 12, 16, 21, 26, 31; G. Douglas Bolton, 6, 8, 25; A. F. Kersting, 7, 15, 28; Sanderson & Dixon Ltd, 14, 18, 19, 20, 30.

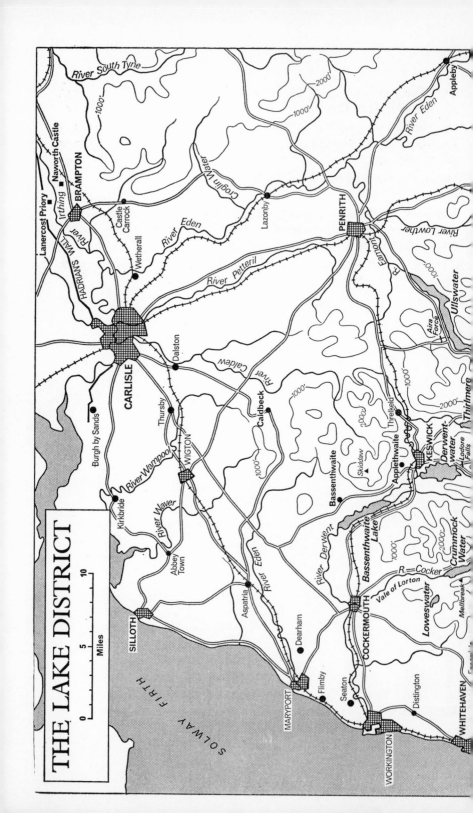

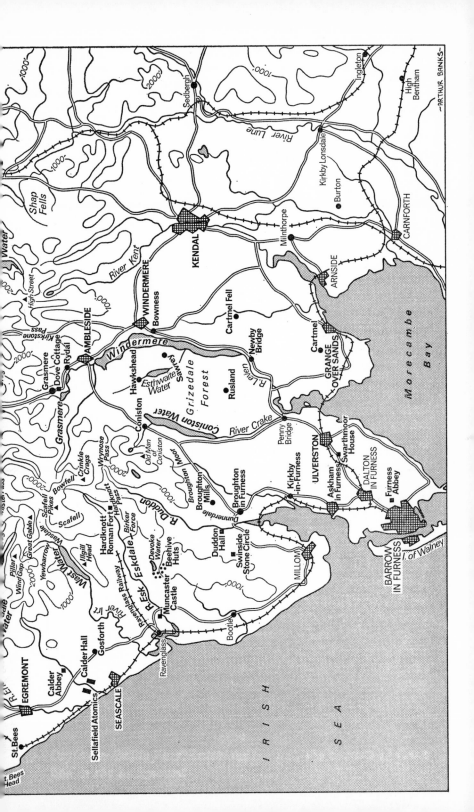

Introduction

I think it likely that few places on earth are more fickle, more blissful, more maddening, more lovely than the English Lake District. Once I heard a shepherd in my dale say: 'Aye, she's fair feckless but gey bonnie.' Why feckless? Because she can change from grey tears to shining laughter in one flick of a misty curtain; and with another flick reduce miles of high splendour to a narrow arc of vague, damp sadness. These wizardries belong to all seasons. They can enchant or irk us at any time of year. And yet the four seasons themselves have distinctive faces, so contrasting that a visitor who has seen the district only in April might hardly recognize the face of October. The colours of early spring are thin and wary, the fell grasses bleached by the frost and nibbled to the sod by sheep; the brackens hiding underground; rowans and larches and spruce shrinking naked against their backcloth of swart rock; lichens drab on the stone walls, and the fells themselves dun and blue-black. Yet under a clear sky this picture has its own cool and pastel splendour, and energetic boots ache to be plodding aloft.

Six months later the fell grasses are tapestries of bright green and lustrous yellow; evil, seductive brackens stipple the slopes with bronze, orange, umber; rowans are traceries of silver and scarlet, and larch needles have a sheen of lemon; lichens vest the walls with gold, rust, emerald. As for the fells, their effect is ripe, benevolent; they appear to have a rich bloom about them. To put it in dale language, the visible difference between April and October is a fair capper; for that matter, so is the difference between July and February.

Introduction

No changes of colour or weather will deter the hardy walker, ready to snatch at any spare tramping days throughout the year. Rain, mist, snow, ice, baking sun and withering winds, tricky crags and dizzy ledges, all are part of the satisfying excitement that channels itself into a kind of euphoria on the long trudge back to the dale. But the majority who visit Lakeland do so in less strenuous fashion; thus I am trying to treat readers of this book as guests of mine. According to what time of year they stay with me I will offer a programme suited to the occasion. A rough and ready calendar is:

Spring—April, May, June
Summer—July, August, September
Autumn (the Back-end)—October, November, December
Winter—January, February, March

The weather in any of these months can be splendid or dreadful, according to individual taste. A snowbound February delights the skier and depresses the lover of warmth. A wet August quite naturally penalizes the mother of the young family and lifts the fisher of sea-trout into ecstasies. On average, May until mid-June, and October, are the driest and sunniest phases, though in 1968, when the South shuddered and soaked, the North-West quivered under four months of hot sun, and the few brief showers were swiftly evaporated by the warm rock.

Whatever the conditions and the time of year, this blend of part-Cumberland, part-Westmorland and North Lancashire has a life that excites decent envy.

Very large numbers of books have been written about it, covering in detail the lions of the district: the lakes themselves; the well-known beauty spots; the walks, the climbs; the ancient buildings; the geology and history of it all. For that reason whole prides of lions have been left out of this account. Skiddaw, Helvellyn, Patterdale, Grizedale, a host of others can take care of themselves. But some places on the way there, or close to them, places for which few trumpets have been sounded, peep shyly into print. So I have called this somewhat personal journal *English Lake Country*.

CHAPTER ONE

Profile

Take a large cloth, soak it in water, bundle it up, and dump it on a table. In a crude fashion the result will bear some semblance to the Lake District, the bulges being the fells, the creases radiating between them the valleys, the water seeping down forming the becks and rivers and lakes. Far back in time the bowels of the earth erupted, the molten lava cooled, the sea made ingress, and then the bed of it was burst open by a second eruption. Glaciers, those vast chisels of the Ice Age, began to fashion the fells as we know them today. They carved the steep slopes, scooped out the hanging valleys, left subsidiary extrusions locally called knots or hows, smaller hills stuck like warts on bigger hills. The final result is an area surprisingly small on the map and astonishingly big to the foot and even to the arrogant wheel.

In the south-west the pinkish-grey granite, purple on a dark, wet day, dominates the scene. Thence onward spread the varied kinds of generic Skiddaw slate, grey-green and elegant at its best, until Threlkeld and then the Shap uplands produce more granite. The western fringes hold coal and iron. Inland more iron, copper, lead, and its alluring handmaiden, silver, have been mined for centuries.

Always the fells and the weather seem to be struggling for mastery. Along the coast the rainfall averages a mere 40 inches. Further inland, as the fells grow taller and colder, they rip the clouds apart, and the average rises to 80, 100, 150, 200 on the summits of Scafell, Gable and their kindred. Then evaporation reduces the temperature, and the mean average at the crown of Scafell equals that of the Alps at 10,000. Here is the sad and simple explanation of why unwary walkers can die from exposure on our fells in seemingly gentle seasons. The best advice is, never judge conditions by the softness of the valleys below; always take rain-proof coverings and extra woollies. To the dalesfolk the weather has a continuous and vital significance. The shepherd intending to go up and gather his flock glances at the sky first thing, reckons the cloud at 2,000, has breakfast. He glances again. The cloud has dropped to 1,500. 'Nay,' he says, 'ah'll bide a bit. Mebbe wait till tomorrow.'

The cool, intense greenery is deceptive. To the casual eye, staring up at billowing emerald, it might appear that the breasts and heights provide enough grazing to feed unlimited sheep and beasts. Much of that lovely herbage is deception. There are seas of bracken, death to cattle and scarcely less dangerous to sheep; exquisite, useless mosses; lichens that once provided dyes and now serve no other purpose than to paint the rocks. In between grow modest grasses, nibbled to the sod in starving early spring. Higher still cling alpine lady's mantle, staghorn mosses, delicate and charming, of use only to reindeer.

Even below, the soil is sparsely rationed over a bed of rock. Crops are a luxury, cattle scarcely more than a hobby except on the richer farms.

What, then, are the main ways of making a living here? First, the hardier breeds of sheep. The toughest, the Herdwicks, will brave the highest peaks in the depths of winter for the sake of minor nibbling. Swalesdales and Cheviots seldom ascend above 2,000 feet in bitter weather. These hill sheep need a maximum of space for a minimum of grazing. A neighbour of mine runs just over 3,000 of them aloft. His fell-grazing stint is 36 miles round. Though that sounds a lot, it has to be augmented in the spring.

Sheep always have been, and likely always will be, the chief industry, though the lesser farms may get absorbed by the greater, a kind of golden handshake arrangement backed by the government. Once upon a time mining ran sheep a good second. Now the large pits on the coast are gradually losing their importance, coal sur-rendering its sceptre to oil, atomic energy, natural gas. One or two iron mines flourish; most are forsaken pink mouths in lonely places. Quarrying has suffered less. Skiddaw slate still brings in money, particularly the green begotten by Honister, lovely to behold and enduring. A roof of this, the topmost slates smaller than postcards, the lowest a foot long, will glorify any building. The silver-grey Kirby slate almost rivals it.

But granite has been losing trade. The pinkish-grey kind from Eskdale no longer surfaces the roads, having given place to ground limestone and bitumen, the friend of every purring car. The monumental masons, too, have rejected granite. An old craftsman said to me: 'It splits too easy. Aye. Thou taps awa', and gits as fur as *In Loving Mem*—and then the boogger cracks. There's nay love aboot that.'

Second place, these days, is held by visitors. In the bleak 1930's they saved the sheep farmer from ruin. In this year of grace, their way eased by such approaches as the M6, they pack the popular centres, and bring their caravans and their tents to quieter spots. On high, life is no less solitary than it was 50 years ago. In full summer I can choose a walk across the fells, a walk of eight hours, with the near certainty of seeing no human being. Where I live, the density of the resident population is one per square mile. But the Lake District, as a whole, courts tremendous popularity, and unlike minor seaside resorts, has a season lasting from March until the beginning of November.

Third in the list is forestry. Its early encroachments were resented with a deal of bitterness. Conifers marched in soulless, rigid patterns up and down the fells around Keswick and Ennerdale. They displaced the sheep-runs, provided more sanctuary for destructive foxes. Nobody loved them. Presently imagination brought about change. Straight lines gave place to curving fringes, screens of hardwood flanked the conifers, splendid ridges were allowed to retain their character by being left un-planted. Some stretches of fell were granted the privilege of beeches, with a few rowans to complete their happiness. The Forestry Commission discovered how to make use of utterly unwanted tracts, marshes such as Foulshaw Moss.

A visitor might well enjoy a day or two cruising past the various plantations, comparing the new with the old. In spring he would see the delicate gems of the larch roses, in late autumn the gold of the larch needles. At any time of year he might catch sight of a buzzard mewing and stalling above, and perhaps, because of its great wing-span, mistake the creature for a golden eagle. A raven could be up there, crying pronk, pronk, and performing a sudden victory roll. Clinging to one of those tall trees could be a foraging pine marten, handsome, savage, creamy of throat, bushy of tail, like some gigantic stoat with a fox's brush. Sometimes the sweet-mart, called thus to distinguish it from its smelly relative, the foum-art or polecat, will leap on to a sheep's back, bite a vein in the neck, and make a meal as the victim collapses from loss of blood. But its rareness somehow palliates such villainy.

CHAPTER TWO

April

Both the coast road and the railway unrolling up West Cumberland are entitled to call themselves blessed. Westward they look across the mouth of the Solway to the blue-grey romance of the Galloway shores. On sharp days they see an etherealized version of the Isle of Man, and even, far, far away, the enticing ghost of the Kingdom of Mourne. Eastward rises the wild surmise of the Eskdale fells, quite incredibly inviting, over the hills and far away to some fairy-tale adventure. This panoply of high granite may be snow-capped in April and the fields flanking the Esk, bereft of pasture by winter and the close-cropping sheep, will loom a pale silvery-yellow, unless spring be extra early. As you stare at the great horse-shoe blocking the eastern sky you will be paying homage to Scafell, the Pike, Esk Pike, Bowfell, Crinkle Crags, in that order, with perhaps a glimpse of Gable to your left and of Harter Fell to your right, Harter the pyramid that somehow suggests a sort of ducal benevolence. Though these things must be a matter of opinion, I swear that this is the loveliest way to approach the Lake District.

From the coast road two lesser roads twine eastward, on either flank of the Esk. Long, long ago, as furtive tracks threading tangled woodland, they must have been trodden by the ancient Britons who fled from their enemies to the sanctuary of the hills. Their fugitive cousins who chose Wales retained a deal of their language, but only a few words have survived here, such as 'pimp', which is five in both Welsh and Cumbrian. The last time I heard it was from the lips of a young shepherd of ours, counting sheep after clipping, 'yan, tyan, tethera, methera, pimp, sethera, lethera, hovera, dovera, dick.' The next to use these tracks were the Romans, and after that a conglomeration including raiding Picts and Scots, and then the Norsemen who truly settled the area and introduced sheep-farming. Sir or Madam, please drive slowly up these dry-walled, winding ways, for the sake of the past, and the present, the ever-present sheep, Cheviots with their noble Roman noses, the black-faced, horned Swaledale, the white-faced, indigenous Herdwick.

There is a third route up the dale, the miniature railway, starting from that former smugglers' lair, Ravenglass. The 15-inch gauge runs for seven and a half miles and gives delight to all nice children up to the age of 80 or so. The first line was constructed in the eighteen-seventies to bring down iron ore. Later it secured the contract to carry Her Majesty's mails, and pictures survive of dignified guards and drivers wearing big beards and small, peaked caps. Financially the line remained close to failure until a few years ago, when a preservation society took it over and sets an example that must be the green envy of nationalized industries. *Vivat* Ratty! (The locals dubbed the narrow gauge the rat-trod, and the diminutive nickname was inevitable.)

At Eskdale Green the Ratty keeps to the south, to avoid the hill upholding the hamlet. But the road sweeps over the crest and passes the bordering wall and the rhododendrons and azaleas of the Outward Bound Mountain School, once the home of Lord Rea. To stand on the terrace there, and look across the lake to the staircase of fells beyond, is to wonder whether this is England or some fanciful setting in Switzerland or Austria. At the end of the terrace kneels a little chapel, triangular, modest, its southern wall entirely of glass. I would like to take the sad, the bitter, the selfish, the envious, the truly wicked, and leave them here for a while to heal their wounds.

Beyond the hamlet the road and the Ratty run as friendly parallels for a distance. This proximity gave rise to a one-sided duel. Two young men I knew, one of them an engine-driver, fell out over a girl. The other, a farm-hand, devised a gorgeous form of insult. He would wait with his push-bike for his rival to appear, driving the engine along this stretch. The speed limit is 15 miles an hour. Pedalling slightly ahead, the farm-hand shouted scurrilous remarks, and the infuriated man in the cab could do nothing about it.

The railway ends at Boot, so tiny as to be missed by a careless eye. At the end of the toy street the Whillan beck racing down from Burnmoor gossips under a hump-backed bridge. 150 yards upstream, in torrential weather, one of the least-known and most frightening waterfalls in the kingdom surges in white, drumming chaos. By strange chance the track above it gives a glimpse of another cascade, almost opposite, cleaving down the fell-breast on the south side of the dale. Birker Force descends about 400 feet through the swart, riven granite, the top of it an overhang. I have known it freeze during a phase of bitter north-west winds, so that the upflung water remains suspended like a giant candelabra.

From Boot onwards Hardknot Pass, some two miles ahead, looms as an exciting challenge or an ominous interdict, according to the temperament of the motorist. Even to the brave, the first visual encounter is something of a shock. As a surfaced road, the worst bit of the pass rivals the steepest in Europe. Narrow, flanked by rock, with a sharp S-bend, to a long wheel-base it presents a gradient of one in two-and-a-half. A faint touch of frost or snow renders it impassable. In winter, with the gorge of the Esk darkly below on one side, the depths of Hardknot Ghyll sullenly beneath on the other, and the menace of Border End black and sheer above, the setting would suit Wagner in his most Gothic mood.

I could write many pages about accidents on Hardknot, some of them, strangely, both bloodless and humorous. The most bewildering occurred one bleak early March. A man spent a Saturday night at a Langdale hotel. On the Sunday morning he told the proprietor he was driving on to the hotel at Wasdale Head, and that there would be no need to book in advance at this empty time of year. He wrote a card, with similar information, to his sister in Shrewsbury. On Tuesday the sister 'phoned the Wasdale Head hotel, only to learn that they knew nothing of her brother. She at once got in touch with the Whitehaven police. They instructed the local police to check up at all inns and farms in Dunnerdale, Eskdale and Wasdale where he might possibly have stayed the Sunday night. Nothing came of inquiries. On the Thursday evening a man from Millom ventured to drive over the pass and saw an ancient car standing unattended on the summit, its windows glazed with hail and snow. That night the police 'phoned and asked me to go up there at crack of dawn. They would, they said, send along a number of police under a sergeant.

The morning was stark, with intermittent blizzards of granulated snow. Four of us locals went up, and some police arrived about half an hour later. Inside the car we found the man's luggage, his hat, a map, and a bag of sweets. The evidence seemed to indicate that he had stopped at the summit for a very brief stroll on the open fell. We reckoned he must have fallen into some nearby gully, and too injured to get back to the car, remained there and died from exposure. In that savage weather a man lying helpless could hardly have survived an hour.

A short, intensive search on either side of the summit revealed nothing. Every so often the world to the east was blotted out by approaching curtains of blizzard. We descended into Dunnerdale for further inquiries, crossed Birker Moor and went back up Eskdale. A 'phone message from police headquarters asked us to make a detailed search of Harter Fell. Also, they wanted the derelict car to be brought down.

That sepia, frigid afternoon we combed Harter without result, and then returned to the summit of the pass. In the twilight a curious cortège descended towards the valley, first a police motor-cyclist, then the ancient car, roped to a police-car behind it lest veteran brakes should fail and kill the constable who had volunteered to steer it. Behind this came a second police car and a civilian saloon holding four of us. One of our party wore a fur hat and an anorak with a fur collar.

By hap a solitary motorist chose to ascend that afternoon from Eskdale. The policeman on the motor-cycle waved him aside, at a spot where the man could stop with safety. Now it happened that about this period the two new, joint dictators of the Soviets, Khrus-chev and Bulganin, had visited England and paid a call on the atomic station at Sellafield, on the coast. The solitary motorist stared with widening eyes at the mobile procession of protective police, caught sight of the fur hat and collar, and in the instant, quite plainly, jumped to the wrong conclusion.

The next morning there arrived more information from Shrewsbury. The missing man was liable to loss of memory, because of an operation on his head the previous year. Most of us began to believe that he had stopped his car on the summit of Hardknot for a breather, taken a stroll, and walked on down to Dunnerdale in deep forgetfulness. By now he might be enjoying a holiday in Cornwall or somewhere afar off, for he carried, said his sister, plenty of money. But we went on searching.

On Sunday morning more folk were available to hunt the fells. Moments before I left with the search party his sister 'phoned, telling me of his particular affection for Esk Hause, that tilted plateau 2,500 feet high, birth-place of the Esk, and notable for the number of people who have gone astray there. Possibly he could have reached Esk Hause, though we shall never know the truth. We found his body on Piet Knot, a spur of Esk Pike, and hoped that he had died quickly.

About 500 feet below the Hardknot summit, on the north side of the road, the power and the glory of Ancient Rome still proclaim themselves. Even those with scant interest in the past will enjoy a visit to the restored ruins of the fort. It was built to protect the convoys passing between Ambleside and Ravenglass, the port selected for the invasion of Ireland, a plan defeated by the failing strength of Rome. When I first knew these ruins they had an evasive fascination. Chunks of stone lay half-hidden in the brackens, though during winter, the greenery flattened by rusty decay, the general outlines of the buildings and defences were clear. Sited on the edge of the Esk Gorge and staring across at the naked, rocky wildness of the Scafells, the steep ghyll of Hardknot on its south side, it would have been easy to defend against the attacks of tribesmen. Yet defence was only part of its purpose. The garrison could be called upon to go out and fight. The Romans had devised offensive-defence 1,700 years before we believed we had invented it in the last war.

In the eighteen-nineties the Cumberland and Westmorland Archaeological Society dug up the encampment, revealing such luxuries as the bath-house with its *sudatorium*, took careful records of all they found, and reburied the past. After the last war the Ministry of Works decided to unearth the whole fort and build the walls up to a certain height. At first I felt annoyed that this high, lonely, haunted place was being interfered with, and as the outline grew more visible, more shipshape, it reminded me of the tidied-up site of a bombed brewery. For years I avoided it, only in the end to realize that the Ministry had brought the fort to life without a scrap of desecration.

To those who stick to the roads, the larger part of Eskdale must remain unknown, for it leaves the road at the base of Hardknot where the beck froths under the bridge, turns its back on wheels and civilization, salutes Brotherelkeld (locally 'Butterilket') farm as the last building in the middle dale, an advanced grange built by the Cistercians to house the brothers who attended the sheep, and saunters away up the Esk Gorge, a narrowness of scree and boulders and stunted grasses walled in by ridges falling steeply, the river itself an excitement of song and foam washing rocks that sometimes look most curiously white. About two miles ahead the hump of Throstlegarth bridge marks the confluence of the Lingcove beck with the Esk. Even the most timid walker could get to the bridge and back without suffering.

At Throstlegarth the upper gorge of the Esk, riving its way down from the left, serves as a barbarous and beautiful prelude to Upper Eskdale. Water flings itself down sheer rock-faces between glistening vertical banks, and the visual is a tapestry of rioting steepness. Beyond the upper gorge the wide, sad marsh of Great Moss sulks between the ruthless flank of Scafell and the remote, untrodden ribs of Esk Pike. This is a place for drama on a huge scale, for terror, tragedy, worship. Dow Crag suddenly emerging from mist could turn a plainsman sick with shock. Here was I involved in my first mountain rescue job, searching in a gale of rain and sleet. Three of us carried the smashed corpse through twilight, two holding the shoulders and the other the legs. I was wearing clogs with steel caulkers, and innumerable stones cluttered the track. Every other step I slipped or stumbled, so at last we took to the marsh itself, until

darkness and the worsening storm brought us to a halt. In the end we covered the body with boulders to protect it from foraging foxes and ravens and buzzards, and returned to the dale to organize a proper carrying party for the next morning.

Birker Moor, which provides the southern barrier to mid-Eskdale, is an ocean of heather surrounding a welter of minor ridges and crags. In a good heather season the fat red grouse scarcely bother to step out of one's way. Not only can they be almost tame but admirably brave. I was once walking here with some friends of mine who had a perky little terrier. It dashed ahead, and put up a cock and hen grouse with their covey of eight youngsters. The cock escorted his wife and children some distance, then suddenly turned and came at the terrier like a flying bomb. I doubt if that dog will ever chase grouse again.

Over the moor runs an excellent road on which sheep choose to sleep in the summer. Local folk driving across after dark have always been on the look-out for ovine sleepers. But some years ago another hazard began to worry motorists. Galloway cattle were becoming popular, because they could stay out all the year grazing on the fells. The matted, broken coat of the Galloway reflects no light. Even its eyes are screened by the hair that masks them. Like the sheep, they cultivated a taste for the road. One cloudy summer midnight I was being driven by a friend who must have extra-sensory perception. He could see no obstacle, but something urged him to stop, and we came to a halt with the bonnet just touching the ribs of a Galloway.

Rightly or wrongly, Eskdale folk believe that Devoke Water, on the far side of the Birker Moor road, belongs to their orbit. In grim weather this isolated lake with its speck of an island lies sullen, secretive. The old boat-house suggests the site of some supernatural horror conjured up by Edgar Allen Poe. Switch to sunshine, the lake becomes a laughing lattice of silver bars, and the boat-house a friendly invitation to pay it a visit. Above the north-eastern flank of Devoke, and on the rising ground just beyond the western end of the lake, the Romano-British selected evacuation areas, a curious activity for those bygone days, but very necessary. The strength

3   *Swaledale sheep in a fold*

of Rome had withered, the troops had gone, and the folk left behind were almost defenceless. Dreading the Picts and Scots and other raiders, certain that if they attempted to stand and fight on the coast they must be defeated by the barbarians, they preferred discretion. Here at the Bronze Age settlement of Barnscar they would be well away from the coast, with long views of any advancing marauders. The remains of about 400 beehive huts are scattered about the neighbourhood of Devoke, some of them granaries. In the spring, before the brackens smother the ground, they are most easy to see; in any event, several are obvious at all seasons, dug up by the Ministry of Works. Perhaps the word archaeology sounds dry. Perhaps to some motorists a short walk on rough ground seems uninviting. Yet to look down at actualities, crude buildings once the homes of one's ancestors, and to say: 'Well, possibly my grandfather to the nth. lived here—' I think that takes the ache out of the rough walk and the dryness out of archaeology.

Back in Eskdale, the yows that have spent their winter on high will have been brought down for lambing. Every farm has its own L-Day, so to speak, when lambing begins, and the nearer the farm stands to the high fells, the later becomes L-Day. The reasons behind this are sound enough, though they can be challenged by the unreliability of the weather, more fickle than any woman. The closer to the fells lie the pastures, the more delayed are the spring grasses. January, February, March are starving months, when a hungry fox will crouch dead-still in a bush for hours, for a mouthful of unsuspecting robin. By late April the natural larder is less empty, and Reynard likely to destroy fewer lambs.

The worst enemy of sheep at this period is the carrion crow. He and his murderous cronies gather on the fringes of the fields, just out of gunshot. Aim a walking stick at him, and he takes no notice. Raise a gun, and he is off in the instant. Woe betide the lamb left unprotected by its mother for a few seconds. A sable murderer flaps down and pecks out an eye or the tongue. Though a fox may slide into a meadow at night and bite off the heads of half a dozen lambs for sport, the crow probably does more damage than the fox.

The April visitor, driving, walking or simply standing and staring, can find fascinating entertainment among the fields of sheep. The lambs themselves, Herdwick, Swaledale, Cheviot, or crosses of these breeds, vary in temperament. Some seem puling, almost helpless. Others have a gaiety, an active sense of humour. Most of them relish an evening romp, a follow-my-leader affair, charging up and down any available banks, and enjoying an occasional stiff-legged aerial leap. There is the petulant whiner, and the robust wanderer. The majority of them choose to sleep for periods on mother's back. When the urge for a feed asserts itself, lamb lifts a tiny hoof and prods mother in the spine.

Now and then an apparently pathetic scene may deceive the kindly visitor. There, on one side of a wall, browses an unheeding yow. On the other side her lamb blares miserably.

'Oh, what a shame!' says somebody. 'The poor little thing wants its feed.'

In fact, mother knows exactly when to pass on the next sucking of milk, and has no intention of spoiling her infant. At the right time she will leap, stick a hoof between the wall stones, and with a second levering to take her over the top, spring down to the other side and feed her child.

Vast numbers of people understand cars. Few, in proportion, have the slightest understanding of beasts or sheep. In a vague fashion they still think of Mary's Little Lamb as a gentle creature that followed her around, meekly subservient to all and sundry. In fact, the average pet lamb grows up to be a swaggering thug, ready to attack man or dog. A friend of mine had a dominating daughter who insisted on keeping a pet lamb. At 18 months it weighed 90 pounds. The dogs gave it a wide berth. It walked about the kitchen, nosed open a cupboard, stole biscuits. A stranger crossing the stackyard was liable to violent assault. It knocked down a boy, attacked a woman who was stepping into her car, and carried out a magnificent joust on a stout old lady who was stooping to fill a bucket—admittedly, an inviting target. My friend grew more and more anxious, positive that the brute would get him involved in a legal case that led to damages for injury. One day I met him looking relaxed and happy.

'How's that vile pet of yours?'

He smiled widely. ''Tis deid! It got at corn bin and bust hissel'.'

Aye, little pet lambs grow up to be big bullies. The yow, too, is far from humble during her phase of motherhood. Once we had as an apprentice a young engineer named George who decided to take up sheepfarming. At lambing time the shepherd taught him how to inject a lamb for pulpy kidney. One afternoon Old Eb and I were mending a wall on a tall bank. We saw George enter a field on his own. He was carrying a hypodermic needle and a bottle of fluid. A rather frowsty yow grazed there with her lamb. The unsuspecting George bent over, to pick up the lamb and inject it. The yow caught him perfectly at the back of the knees, and over he went, face downwards into a sloshy patch.

Eb nodded appreciatively. 'That's t'way to larn.'

Nearer to the coast the sheep become fewer and the beasts and the crops more noticeable. The Esk winds its way down to the sea between Birkby Fells and Muncaster Fell, this latter a small, narrow and charming barrier, much earlier with its display of greenery than the taller, more inland heights. Where the skirts of it slope down to the south-west, the coast road crosses the river by a shallow stone bridge. Across the gap, above a wide terrace, looms the bulk of Muncaster Castle, and further along the ridge, to the east, its original pele tower points at the sky. Not so long since a sizeable tree was growing out of the tower, and when gales swept the neighbourhood I wondered whether the wildly swaying tree would bring the tower crashing into ruin. Now the tree has been removed, and the pele should be safe for many more centuries.

Of the rebuilt castle I have little to say, but to the gardens no superlatives could do justice. Even in the earliness of April there is colour. During May and the beginning of June the great walls of rhododendron and azaleas have no parallel in the kingdom. This is not merely because of their massed and almost luminous tinting. They and the emerald terrace look up the whole romantic valley of Eskdale to the most adamant and desolate fells in Lakeland. The contrast is extraordinary. At your feet, velvet turf, flanked by flowering shrubs and exotics. About you, rhododendrons and azaleas on a Himalayan scale. Below you, the platinum twinings of the Esk, a pastoral bowl to your left where cattle drowse, and to your right the estuary opening upon the Irish sea: full eastward, barren crags unchanged since the molten lava cooled into sterile hardness.

I have a friend, a worshipper of gardens, who stayed with me one May.

'You ought,' I said, 'to visit Muncaster.'

He shook his head. 'No, thanks. Every year, in its proper season, I stay at Bodnant for a fortnight. The most beautiful of all gardens. I don't want to look at anything less.'

I could, of course, have been rude. It was tempting. However, I went on suggesting gently that Muncaster really was quite an idea if he had nothing else to do, and eventually persistence won, and he went off in a reluctant fashion.

He came back terribly late. He stared at his feet. He fiddled with his pipe. He sniffed, and dabbed with his handkerchief, and gave out little mumbles.

Then he said in a strangled tone: 'It's better than Bodnant.'

The Penningtons, Earls of Muncaster, were formerly lords of Pennington, in north Lancashire, centuries before the Norman conquest. At Muncaster their nearest equals south of them, the Huddlestones, lived at Millom Castle, a family who held the ultimate power of *jura regalia* and hanged offenders on their own gallows. A pretty young Pennington daughter, Helwise, with no say of her own in those arrogantly male medieval days, was betrothed to Sir Ferdinand Huddlestone. The poor child loved Dick, one of her father's woodcutters. I expect she slipped out unseen occasionally, to cling to him among the masking leafage and wish with all her heart that she had been born a village lass.

Nearby they held an annual fair. Dressed obscurely, she dared to attend the fair and dance with Dick. Somebody recognized her, and the offensive news reached Sir Ferdinand. In his eminence it was unthinkable that he should take direct personal action. So he let it be known, quietly, that whoever cared to bring Dick's head to him would receive a bag of gold.

The professional jester employed by the Penningtons knew Dick's routine—a morning of woodcutting, a break for his food and a nap beneath a shady tree, before another stint of felling. The jester waited until his victim was asleep, grabbed the axe, severed his head and took it to Sir Ferdinand.

Helwise, it seems, somehow recovered the head. Drenching it with her tears, and kissing those cold lips, she stumbled up to the summit of Muncaster fell, which rears itself nearly opposite the castle, on the far side of the road ascending from Ravenglass. There she buried the head, and forsaking the everyday world that no longer offered anything but grief, became a bride of Christ.

At Muncaster we are on the fringe of the Lake District proper, though still well within the dominion of the fells, for ten miles south Black Combe spreads its determined bulk, a bull of a mountain where bilberries abound, to stain the legs and mouths of the browsing sheep. Few visitors come to its generous summit. The last time I was there, in a thin mist, a pair of peregrines allowed me to approach within 40 yards. In crystal weather the view includes a sweeping parade of fells, an almost measureless coastline, the Irish sea, the Isle of Man, the Solway and the Mull of Galloway. As for its half-circle of black crags overlooking the Whicham valley, to squat on the edge stirs feathers in a nervous stomach. It has a quality of warning about it. The last time but one I was there, with a friend, we sat uneasily on a bit of rock at the top to nibble our lunch.

He looked down and said: 'D'you know, if this was sheer, instead of just very steep, I don't believe it would be so frightening.'

Next he said: 'I always like to start with an apple,' drew one from his rucksack, and let it slip. Its downward progress was peculiarly macabre.

If you seek out Black Combe, visit Waberthwaite Church on the way there or on the way back. Travelling south on the coast road, drive slowly when nearing the top of the hill beyond Muncaster Bridge. A signpost proclaims Hall Waberthwaite. The lane twines down in wayward leisure, past a few sleepy farms, until it reaches the bank of the Esk, here a semi-estuary. The church with its acre of tombstones above the water belongs to another world. Grey, plain, immensely solid, with box pews, it suggests some ancient and not quite truthful etching.

Nearly 20 years ago a friend of mine was buried there on a sunny afternoon in May. All the local folk had liked him, and they attended in force. Many of the mourners were old men over 80. They wore black mourning suits tailored in the eighteen-nineties, the jackets and waistcoats buttoning high up to the knot of the tie, the trousers tubular, their bowlers of similar period. They stood there talking in the churchyard while a light, salty breeze from the sea ruffled the daffodils, and on the muddy edge of the estuary shelduck waddled with a gleam of amber and drifting curlews called to the tolling of the bell.

I felt that I had fallen out of Time, and the feeling was far from unwelcome.

CHAPTER THREE

May

Although we hail May as a truly festive month, once in an evil while cold winds, and perhaps grey skies as well, make nonsense of the claim. Then the primroses and bluebells and violets seem unwilling to leave the darkness of the hard earth, and the cunning brackens remain in hiding until they can be almost certain of escaping frost. But if you are passing from Eskdale (Eshd'l, the dale of water, in local language) to Wasdale in a benign May, go slowly. Only a pagan would flash past the white sprays of the bird-cherry bedecking the road-banks and clustered in tall, pale beckonings along the skirts of the fell. Here and there the walker will meet a whitebeam. A few hundred yards upstream of Eskdale Church, which might have grown out of the river bank, the track passes a piece of old, low walling on the south. Behind it, among other trees, a whitebeam holds up silver leaf-buds that seem to float independently, like soap bubbles. As a Japanese print it would rank among the unbelievable.

Before you reach Wasdale, even before you have unwillingly escaped from Eskdale, there is a demure turning to the right by the side of three elegant stone cottages, the nearest bearing the badge of the Cumberland and Westmorland Constabulary. It could equally have served Beatrix Potter, as an illustration for one of her stories. Crime? Offence? Oh, nonsense! Not here. A shapely little stone house and a garden full of flowers. Very suitably the turning leads into a toy dale, Miterdale, threaded for a mile or two by a narrow road leading to a bridge over the Mite. Beyond this a rough way for wheels dies at Low Place, the final farm.

May

I have heard visitors, in sunshine, almost purring as they walked the upper reaches of the Mite, first along this bank, then the other, the water shimmering, whispering, splashing over rocks and pebbles, the sides of the dale pressing closer, the great bulk of Scafell blocking the view ahead. I have heard visitors, in dreary weather, muttering something about not caring for the spot, and seen their legs quicken, watched their expression twist into distaste. How can something that happened long years since imprint itself on the innocence of an untouched valley?

Miterdale used to shelter a number of homesteads and an inn. The ruins of them hide among the old trees on the north bank. Here the packhorse trains, on their journeys from Keswick through Wasdale Head, passed down to Miterdale, and on to the coast. Wheels began to displace the packhorse, and iron mining near the coast lured the younger generations from the dale. The inn closed, started to crumble; one after another the steads became empty. At last only a single farmhouse survived, Miterdale Head, occupied by a middle-aged farmer and his young wife and their baby.

On an autumn Thursday he set off for Whitehaven market by cart. He said: 'If ah's not back be six, ah'll be stayin' night yonder. So lock oop t'spot.'

'Oo, aye.'

In the later afternoon his wife was making tallow dips, drawing the pith from seeves, tubular reeds, and dipping them in a cauldron of boiling sheep fat. Every so often she looked out to see if her husband were in sight. At twilight she took a final glance. To her surprise she saw a distant figure, not coming up the dale from the seaward side, but down from the moor. Waiting, she discerned a tall, gaunt woman, her head swathed in a scarf. The visitor said she had left Keswick to visit relatives nearer the coast, that she had lost herself on Burnmoor, that she was tired and hungry. Could she have a meal and a bed for the night?

The farmer's wife disliked the look of her, but Cumbrian hospitality took charge. She invited the woman in, offered her as a seat the sconce by the side of the fire, turned to prepare a meal. The contrast of the heat after the cold made the visitor drowsy. She fell asleep, and her head drooped, and the scarf slipped off, and her jaw sagged. When the farmer's wife came over to say the meal was ready, her appalled eyes saw not a woman, but a man with a vile face. Positive he had used this disguise to get inside for the purpose of robbery, and with no help to be had for miles, she almost gave way to her first impulse, to snatch up her baby and run. But there was nowhere to run except the darkening, cold fell; and she dreaded that the slightest movement might awaken the marauder to murder. Desperate, she thrust the ladle into the boiling fat and tipped it down his open throat. A second tipping of the ladle was enough. When the farmer returned next morning he found a demented wife and a tallow choked corpse on the floor.

Twelve years ago a friend of mine discovered an ancient yellow newspaper among the rubbish in the attic. It reported a crime in Whitehaven. Two seamen landing from a brigantine had quarrelled on the quay, one stabbing the other to death. The murderer had made for the fells. Later, while a farmer and his wife were out, their isolated farmhouse had been broken into and some of her clothes stolen. Here was the dreadful answer to the puzzle.

The sconce was used in Low Place until 1967. The ruins of the inn, where the Miterdale farmer buried the woman-man, still huddle among the brackens on the north bank. Along this stretch, on a sombre day, people with no knowledge of the story tend to look over the shoulder and quicken their pace. Those who do so can find brightness and buoyancy. The road to Santon Bridge and dale climbs airily over the breast of Irton Pike, and there the Irish Sea fills the visible west. A sharp turn to the right below is a meek introduction to a road view ahead, the summit of a moderate hill that flings the scene wide open, Wastwater and its insistently fierce bodyguard of fells, the black cliffs of the Screes, Scafell Pike, Gable, Kirk Fell, dizzy Yewbarrow, the uncaring crags of Buckbarrow where I saw cragfast foxhounds being rescued by a young huntsman balanced on a ledge and pushing them up over his head.

In May the delightful thought of an old lady shines among the Forestry Commission's plantations to the right of the road. She sold the ridge for planting, but insisted that one prominent rib should be

4 *Looking down Wrynose Pass to the reverse slopes of Hardknot and Harter*

coloured with rhododendrons. Here I saw a surprised woman tourist blow them a kiss.

The doorstep to Wastwater is gentle Nether Wasdale. Had Herrick lived later and been an architect instead of a poet, I think he would have designed the vicarage. A dear old soul I knew for long years had a bosom friend living in this hamlet. Call them Hannah and Maggie. Maggie, honest, decent, but no Helen of Troy, was due to be wed in her early twenties, and Hannah had been chosen as her bridesmaid. The vital day arrived, the sacred ceremony to begin at one o'clock. At twelve Hannah went round to the bride's house to help with her dressing. She found the girl wearing her everyday clothes and a sacking brat, or apron. It was puzzling, and as the clock ticked on and Maggie made no move, Hannah could bear it no longer.

''Tis twenty past,' she said, 'and thou's to be wed at one. Gaa oop and git changed.'

Maggie took her by the arm, led her to the window, pointed at the long, winding trod descending the face of Mecklin Fell. Her bridegroom, an Eskdale bobbin-turner, was expected to arrive by this track.

She said: 'Ah's doin' nowt till ah see him. Ah's been made a fool of yance (once) before.'

These days Wastwater grows popular. Yet the way from Nether Wasdale to the lake itself always seems peaceful. Before the Screes rear up in dark ferocity there spreads a green ridge wounded by a pink gash. This ravine, named Hall Ghyll, is the last assertion of Eskdale granite, with which the weather has played grotesque tricks. Among the natural sculpturings are pinnacles and a coronet. East of the ghyll the Screes suddenly assault the eye with their fierce cliffs.

Towering, cracked, unrelenting, the enormous rock wall of the Screes crowned by Ilgill Head, 2,000 feet high, looks brutal. Even the fanning scree slopes, suggestive of Goya's fashionable ladies, offer a hint of menace, of potential avalanche. From the road flanking the north edge of Wastwater the cliffs appear to plunge straight into the lake; in fact, a track gropes painfully along the base of them, a knobbly, scrambling, beastly pilgrimage. A friend of mine took his wife walking there, and when she could find sufficient breath, she said: 'If you ever do a thing like this again, I'll divorce you.'

Wasdale Hall, by the foot of the lake, faces the most hostile stretch of the Screes. Now owned by the National Trust, it was built and originally occupied by a private banker. In howling winds, in greyness, in sad rain, it has a haunted look. This is hardly surprising, for the place has failed to shake off a tragedy that shadowed it in the reign of George the Fourth. The lovely young wife of the owner went out one day, leaving her child in the care of the governess. Somehow the child slipped away unseen, fell into the lake, and was drowned. They recovered the tiny body and put it on the bed in a double room that looks at the Screes. The mother returned to be met with the awful news, and was never able to come to terms with her grief.

People ignorant of the story have met her in strange places. Two young women I know, sceptics with both feet on the ground, were walking the track that borders the top of the Screes one hot morning. Coming towards them appeared a pretty young woman and a child dressed in the costume of the eighteen-twenties. They took it to be eccentricity until they glanced again and saw nothing. A young man and his wife, equally ignorant of the story and equally hard-headed, had a similar experience up there. Again, it was a warm, golden day.

A man of charm and integrity, whose father bought the Hall just after the First World War, told me that as a boy of 13 he was put in that double room. He never saw anything, but cold terror so racked him, he had to be moved to another. His elder sister occupied it for two nights, and then refused to enter it again. His younger sister endured one night of it. Then there came to stay with them an aunt whom he described as 'a bit of a battle-axe'. She was given the room, and roused the household in the small hours by her terrible screaming. They found her in the long corridor, nearly gibbering in panic. She said she had woken up, and the room was full of moonlight, and there by the window, staring out at the Screes, stood a young a woman in costume of the 1820's. She was about to say: 'How dare you walk into my bedroom!' when the young woman turned, crossed to the bed, and looked down, her face racked with an agony of grief.

The man of integrity put forward a theory. There were some, he suggested, who could never master their sorrow in life, and remained earthbound after death. Poor young Mrs. Rawson! Poor child! Their spirits may be about the Hall. Their bodies are in Nether Wasdale churchyard.

As a light-hearted contrast there is the modern cattle-grid on the road, a little way beyond the Hall. When it was first constructed I spent a whole delicious afternoon watching sheep egging one another on to cross the obstruction. Small, tentative hoofs dabbed at the bars. Besides the usual whickerings there were furtive ovine grunts, snippets of advice, I swear, from the more cunning yows. By four o'clock, they had mastered the obstruction and with little blares of triumph were reaching the other side. The authorities had to instal a new grid with revolving bars. The affair reminded me of a farmer I met further north, in a wild and what might be dubbed out-of-date area. Surprisingly, he had a grid on his farm-road. To the representative pouring out sales talk on the subject he had said he doubted if the thing would work.

'O.K.,' said the traveller. 'Let us put it in. If it doesn't work, you don't pay.'

That seemed fair enough. The grid was constructed, and that autumn the farmer put it to a crucial test. It was the breeding season, the tups chained in pairs by their horns to prevent them leaping the walls and rampaging up the fells in Don Juan enthusiasm before the proper time. He unchained his tups, left them on one side of the grid. He gathered his yows from the fell and left them on the other side.

At that point in his story he looked at me squarely. 'Ah said: "Noo, git on wi'it, you —s." But they couldna. So ah paid bill.'

The word 'dramatic' has been so abused, I hesitate to apply it to Wastwater. Its three and a half miles of deep water below a tall barricade of fells must have looked biblically impressive at any season a century ago. Whether the sun shone on the silent nakedness, or cloud hid the tops of the Screes or filled the hollow with threatening gloom, there must have been that sense of isolation, stern banishment from the everyday world. Even now, in the dead parts of the year, Wastwater comes into its desolate splendour. But during popular periods, when moving cars and parked cars form a sort of painted metal rim along the edge, a hermit pulls up the skirts of his gown or tucks his trousers into his socks and goes off to hide himself among the crumpled heights. Scenery that owns a road is bound to pay the penalty of beauty these days. I often think that nice London folk who seek to escape their fellows on a Sunday by making for the Surrey hills or the Sussex downs might do better in Cannon Street.

As far as I know, Wastwater never freezes except along its fringes. Whooper swans come here in the winter, yacking like sheep-dogs. It can be rough at any time, with malicious currents. An October morning, glittering of sky and flailed by a continuous east wind, saw myself and a friend ascending the Greendale beck and gawping back every minute or so at the lake performing a weird watery rite. With utter precision of timing, curtain after curtain of spray, at least 60 feet high, kept sliding down to the west. The mechanical regularity of it was almost indecent. Higher up the trod we met a local chap, and expressed our wonder in superlatives.

He said: 'Nay, 'tis nowt. Ah's seen it twice that high.'

People with romantic minds should come along here early on a still summer's morning. The reflections in the lake at this time are such that a photograph of it, held upside down, shows an identical likeness. A dalesman vowed to me that a crony of his who lived near Loweswater, and failed to sleep off all the effects of a certain night before, believed he was walking into the woods there and stepped into the lake instead.

The road along Wastwater must have been pretty rough prior to the motor-car. I was shown an old print dating from the 1830's. Gable frowned in the background like the wrath of God. The road was a ribbon of rock and dust. In the foreground a young man led a horse, its passenger an attractive girl riding side-saddle. Her dress was the conventional style of the period, rather elaborate for such remoteness. The young man wore a type of Tyrolean hat, his jacket draping his shoulders with the effect of a cloak, and shorts. In my ignorance I put this down to artistic licence, only to be told by someone who had studied the subject that I was wrong. Those days, said my informant, young dalesmen wore leather shorts made out of sheepskin. The wool inside served as underpants, unless the wearer was so hard up as to clip it away and sell it for a penny or two. Myself, I would have preferred the clipped style. The wool must have tickled like the very devil.

About half way along the lake, where the Netherbeck comes exulting down among rocks and ferns and silvery, festive rowans, a bridge and a pinkish stone monolith mark the near boundary of the parish of Bowderdale, now, I imagine, a name rather than a title of authority, since its only building is Bowderdale Farm. About half a mile further on another bridge, crossing the Overbeck, and another monolith mark the far boundary. I hope the crowded cities cast no envious eye on Bowderdale. Its guardian angel, Yewbarrow, appears at this angle to be the steepest fell in the Lake District. Though no rope is needed, a steady head, careful feet and a light breakfast are assets.

The first occasion I was on Yewbarrow I happened to glance across at the lip of the Screes opposite washed by the early evening light. A pattern resembling two sides of a triangle marked a particularly steep tilt. Staring, I made out that the pattern was a bit of old wall, built of the rough stones scattered around up there. Isaac Newton might have wondered how it remained standing. The gradient was a challenge to his theories. The absurdity of the wall's existence bewildered me, until I learned of the Parish Award. In far off days this was sponsored by the government. It was up to the various dales to reach agreement about their fell-grazing stints. Once they had settled their boundaries, the government would pay for the legal costs. But if the dalesmen wanted to build dividing walls, that was their own affair.

Eskdale claimed a sterile half-acre, too sterile to feed a single rabbit, on the lip of the Screes. The men who built that wall could never have heard of danger money, but they certainly deserved it.

In winter, Wasdale Head holds a suggestion of the ultimate. A tiny bowl crowded about by unrelenting fells, its sunlight is brief, since the morning shadows stay late and the evening shadows come early. A plainsman first visiting here on a January day might want to head straight back for the coast, scared off by the oppression of the rock. On this side Scafell and her brother, the Pike, are adamant dictators, and the skirts of Pillar and Red Pike turn the basin of Moasdale into a witch's cauldron.

A fine May softens the scene. A little way up the Moasdale track larch-roses purse their young pink lips. Great inclines of fell sprawl green-gold under the sun, so vivified by the contrast of the shadows, they might be providing their own light. The way up the Sty is a friendly invitation. If you accept it, pause at the church. The churchyard is a forlorn little reminder that men are frail and rocks merciless. Of the few buried here, the majority met their death above. Are men fools to pit themselves against mountains, with the risk of falling off into eternity? What shall be said of the actual fall? In my youth I pitched down about a hundred feet. Below, a deep bank of fluffy snow provided undeserved survival. During the drop itself all I knew was an angelic sense of freedom.

Before the church was consecrated, just after the turn of the century, the dead were taken either to Nether Wasdale or St. Catherine's, Eskdale. Mourners in winter had to be well-wrapped and sturdy to follow the pack pony carrying the coffin over the cold wastes of Burnmoor. There were mishaps. Up out of Wasdale Head on its last journey was born the body of a young man, only son of an elderly couple. Half way across the moor the pony took fright, and bolted into the gathering murk with the coffin. The mourners searched in vain, and their dire news was a final blow to the mother, already in decline. She died a week or two later. Again a small funeral cortège plodded up to Burnmoor, the wind moaning, the fells masked in gun-metal mist. The man leading the pony held on tightly, and yet once more there was sudden, frantic shying and the pony broke loose. This time the searchers told themselves they dared not fail, and spread out to comb the fractured breasts of Great How. Hours later they caught the first pony, still bearing the son's coffin. The other pony carrying the dead mother was never seen again. Local folk reckoned it had perished in Quagrigg Moss, half marsh, half peat-hag, smeared between Great How and the western flank of Scafell. Now and again, on gloomy days, somebody reports having seen a spectral pony galloping over the moor, hoofs striking rock and scree without sound, but sending up sparks.

A relief from this grim legend is the tale of the Wasdale Head farmer whose spouse made life a misery with her nagging. She died, and on a rough bit of the moor the pony stumbled, the coffin dropped off and broke open, and the woman sat up, having been only in a trance. The disappointed husband took her home. A month or two later she died once more. Everyone was positive about it. But during this second funeral, as the pony approached the rough stretch, the widower hurried in front, turned, raised imploring arms, and cried: 'Lads, thou maun be gey carefu' here.'

Anybody who chooses to potter for a while will find two passes not far beyond the church. The higher, the new Sty, wanders mainly among rock and loose stone. Vicious winters disrupt it, gripping and swelling with their frost until the thaw sets in, and the track disintegrates into loosened chaos. One May, after a long, fierce winter, I had to ascend a part of the Sty on my hands and knees. The pebbles and small boulders and flakes of rock were piled at trigger balance. It so happened that the same evening I picked up a book by that splendid writer of fiction, A. E. W. Mason. Called *A Romance of Wasdale*, it was, I believe, his first novel. Later he tried to withdraw it from circulation, wanting to suppress the honourable blunders of the beginner. The heroine lived at Keswick. The hero, fair and blue-eyed, was staying at Burnthwaite Farm. The villain, black-moustached, and with flashing white teeth, had a room at the Wasdale Head Inn. One night the heroine saddled her pony and unbeknown to her parents, set off for the Sty. Utterly in the villain's power, she was riding over the pass in pitch blackness to plead with him.

At this stage of the story I began to giggle, because, to my mind, the author was writing rubbish. A girl riding the Sty by night would break her neck. I mentioned it to an old daleswoman, and received a deserved rebuke. Before the days of cars, she said, the county authorities kept parties of men at both ends of the Sty to maintain it in good order.

I was guilty, too, of another blunder. Mason's heroine might have chosen the old Sty, an easy trod meandering over greenish hillocks and along by the beck. Motorists in thinnish shoes who incline towards a mild walk should sample a portion of this route.

Even a dalesman is inclined to forget the old, lonely ways made across the fells, five hundred, a thousand years ago. Those ancients had the engineering knowledge, the strength of arm and skill of hand to build drift-roads, terraced with stone on the lower side, which took them and their beasts and sheep from one dale to another without too much struggle. Stretches of them can still be found in stony and splintered desolation, places that might strike the wanderer today as never having known the foot of man.

Not long since, the manager of the Ratty unearthed a time-table of 1879. One entry was the curious announcement 'Boot (for Wasdale Head).' He came to me and asked if I could make any sense of it. Admittedly, a traveller alighting at Boot could reach Wasdale Head by trudging six miles over Burnmoor, but it seemed, at the least, a very misleading under-statement. Mentioning this to a farmer's wife who had lived at Wasdale Head as a child, she nodded and said: 'Aye, 'twas so in them days.'

Until the coming of the car, she explained, the corpse road between Boot and Wasdale was maintained at a standard good enough for a cart to rumble over it. As a young girl she herself had ridden that way. Her information made me want to lift my hat to the memory of those workmen; considering that the Wasdale end of the moorland track today claws its descent down terraces of awkward rock where waterfalls gush across in rainy weather, I marvel how they tamed Nature and forced her to yield a passage for horse and cart.

6 *Great Gable and the road to Wasdale Head*

CHAPTER FOUR

June

On the way from Wasdale to Calderbridge, the most uncompromising atheist should visit Gosforth church, to praise the Runic Cross. All along West Cumberland the transition from the Dark Ages to the return of Christianity is recorded in enduring stone. Whenever I stand and stare, remembering that somebody else must have stood and stared at the same thing a full thousand years ago, I long for a brief return to those days; only brief, for life must have been full of alarms, raiders, wolves, and other discomforts. But it would be exciting to have a short peep at Norsemen with winged helmets and long golden hair, ravagers and settlers who have left their language embedded in the local tongue.

Calderbridge proffers a serene escape from the main road. The contrast between turning to the east and turning to the west cannot really be measured by any words. Westward is the atomic world of Sellafield and Calder Hall, eastward the world of sheep, the newest next to the oldest trade known to man. Two immense towers and a shimmering dome are the symbols of nuclear energy. Years ago there was a scaring occasion when radio-active vapours poured out of those towers, and the press headlines were pregnant with local doom. Police visited the farms with stern notices. 'All milk must be poured into special containers, which will be removed by the atomic authority.' This must be done and that must be done, and so forth. Two solemn constables came to us at eight in the morning.

'Woudsta care fur a sup o' tea?' said Eb.

7 *On Great Gable: Kern Knotts on the left, the summit of Great End in the background*

They nodded and answered: 'Aye.'

'Wi' contaminated milk?'

'Aye.'

No harm came to them, nor to the close-cropping sheep, thought to be incurring grave danger from the infected herbage. Wiseacres said: 'Ah, but wait and see. The second generation—the third generation—.' There were prophecies of malformed lambs, monstrosities, mutterings about heavy claims for damages. But nothing happened, sheep being unable to read newspapers.

Turn east, and—I mean this with reverence—there is the peace of God that passeth all understanding. A half-forgotten road hides between fields and parkland, the ancient meadows and veteran trees of Calder Abbey, an offshoot of the parent foundation at Furness. Intoning gently nearby is the river Calder. Trees have lodged on the high arches of the pink and grey ruin and somehow drawn life out of the dead stonework. The sculpturings of the masonry, the tapestries of mosses and wild flowers on the walls, the fallen slabs with their phantoms of incised lettering, the approach beneath trees that are Goliaths by Cumbrian standards, the quietude composed of grassy whispers and subdued bird-song, the benevolence of the vale itself merging into green space, these belong to a Victorian picture, painted or written, or early Medieval romance. It might have been deplorably otherwise, but for the Rymer family, who out of their own pockets saved what was left of the abbey.

As the road narrows further on beneath a tall, wooded bank it crosses a sandstone bridge where every self-respecting car should stop, for its owner to lean over the parapet and bow to the artistry of those who made it. Further on again, the road becomes gated, and there is a notice, BEWARE OF THE BULL. The last time I was here, with a companion who looked askance at the words, I said casually, 'Oh, don't worry. That board's as old as the hills. Never been a bull in my time.'

He stared and pointed. 'Then what's that?'

I swallowed and said: 'It's a bull.'

A fine big brute it was, uninterested in cars, and we drove along the fell road to the isolation of Thornholme, an old grey farm run by pleasant folk. Far below glittered the Calder in its wide, deep, wooded gorge. We walked down the trod to its junction with Worm Ghyll, crossed the footbridge, and went up a diagonal track ascending north-east. Right over this upland area, across Stockdale Moor, spread the megalithic ruins that must once have been an impressive settlement. Neither of us knew the slightest thing about the subject. Perhaps that was all to the good. Archaeologists, I find, are fierce people where their work is concerned, and refuse to pander to imagination. The two of us had a lovely day, plodding through brackens, squelching among mosses, drifting from ruin to ruin, some surprisingly large, and offering each other our untrained theories. The green and gold world of slope and counterslope was ours; we conjured up exciting, ignorant speculations; rested often; drowsed now and then under the lark-like trilling of meadow-pipits. I must have drifted off once into real sleep, for when I awoke I believed I was in the Scottish lowlands, so like to them is this Calder country and so different from the craggy domination of Eskdale and Wasdale.

Returning to Calder Abbey, a sharp little hill almost opposite turns north out of the valley road. Fifty odd yards up the slope it splits, the right fork to Cold Fell, the left to Haile. On this way to Haile the fields were Rymer country, and here they did something so astonishing, I hesitate to tell other folk, feeling like an angler who has caught an eight-foot salmon and simply dares not utter such an untruth. If you disbelieve me, go up there in early June. You can see for yourself that they planted laburnum along the roads and along the field hedges, high bowers of laburnum, some of it now between 20 and 30 feet tall. How they dissuaded the beasts from grazing on this fatal loveliness I know not, but there to this day are the pendant showers of bloom, and there are the cattle, and there are no tales of sickness or sudden death. From here to Haile, along the skirts of Cold Fell, dawdling is a virtue, and Haile itself, despite its iron mine, remains green and dreamy.

Not far off, by the town of Egremont, protrude more workings, of rich kidney ore. A friend living there invited me to stay for the week-end. On the Sunday night he said he had arranged a trip down the Florence mine for the next morning. I thought his choice of the noun rather frivolous. At ten on Monday we went along to the mine manager's office, where I was issued with overalls and a helmet. I said to my friend : 'But—where are yours?'

He shook his head. 'I'm not going down. I've a horror of hearing a sudden explosion.'

Before my panic could express itself the manager bustled me into the cage with a foreman, who said, 'Thou's a stranger, so t'chaps 'll joke a bit. Pay no heed.'

We dropped 900 feet very fast, and stepped out into a broad shaft lit by electricity. Along the walls the kidney ore resembled bunches of grapes. Ascending a ladder slimy with red hematite I slipped, fell back on the floor of the level, and became a sight that would have frightened Macbeth. There is this to be said, that mines such as the Florence are palaces compared with the wicked, uncaring little tunnels our ancestors bored deep into the fells.

Back at the junction of the Haile and Cold Fell turnings, the road to the right takes its time to ascend, crosses a grid, and reaches the open fell. Whins skirting the road have the shape of plump, neat cushions. Westward the Solway and the Irish Sea spread wider and wider. On a sharp day, between the Mull of Galloway and Man, rises the far hump of Mourne. Rarely, and miraculously when it happens, the Sugar Loaf mountains below Dublin pierce the south-western horizon. Eastward the fells roll upward with a kind of genial laziness, and at their skirts are farms with names far removed from the everyday world, Skalderskew, Farmery.

The trees of the Forestry Commission on Cold Fell are young yet, and the area they occupy looks slight compared with the billows of naked land. A toy valley, Uldale, a child's conception, creeps below the trees. Up above, on the right of the road, a toy circle of standing stones provides a note of mystery. And then there comes the dip down to Ennerdale, a country of crags, water, woods, wandering lanes. Along one of these, a notice board giving warning of its narrowness, a friend and I took a big car. Our silliness earned reward instead of penalty. Around a snake-like curve we met a beautiful old dowager of a steamroller in the employ of the Ennerdale Rural

June

District Council. On her breast the rampant horse shone like some order of chivalry. Over her stretched a scalloped canopy, and I think her name was Emma. It was a sun-drenched morning, the lake a long glitter below the piled fells, the dewy grasses still sleepy, and we both felt how strange and satisfying it was that Emma should fit so perfectly into her surroundings. Fortunately for us a pocket of spare ground enabled her to move off the road, and as we passed my friend swore that she gave us a curtsy.

The walk round the lake includes variety and excitement. Starting from the weir near Crag Farm, a track runs innocently for a while above the level of the water. Presently, Angler's Crag, where the *chak, chak* of the merlin may be heard, changes the opinion of the walker. The way grows high, narrow, airy, steepness dropping to the left, and a hump ahead might be the prelude to empty space. John Bunyan would have compared it with the difficult approach to Heaven. Take courage, scramble over, slither down the scree, and listen to three whistling cheers from a sandpiper, or later, among the trees, to the wooden clacking of ring ouzels. You can now walk safely and flatly, perhaps a little oozily, to the footbridge over the Liza. On this north side, edged by a road, the lower fells are smothered by trees almost up to Black Sail Youth Hostel. They were planted in the early years of the Forestry Commission, blotting out the biggest sheep-run in the Lake District, and merited criticism tinged with sulphuric acid. Now the anger is dead, and the trees, for all their monotony, seem to belong. My sole complaint would be that to walk among them, down from Black Sail to Gillerthwaite, on a humid summer's afternoon, is to run the painful gauntlet of clegs and midges. Clegs, as Eb says, is gey vicious. He tells the story of a haytime occasion, these horse-flies at their most savage. One alighted on his fore-arm. About to swat it, in the interests of science he refrained and watched, saw the thing move up to softer flesh near the bicep. There it straddled its legs for a firmer stance, lifted its proboscis, honed it well, reared back and then swung forward with a terrific stab.

Insect deterrents sold by the chemists are better than nothing. Another method is to wear a sprig of bracken in the hat, the pests

53

buzzing about the tip of the sprig instead of one's face. This particularly applies to flies. An unclean pipe charged with black twist can make them think twice. And there is the exotic method of carrying a tame chameleon on one's shoulder.

A short way down on this side of the lake a beck cleaves through the woodland, its companion a rough track. It provides gentle, sauntering access to the open fell, and after ten minutes or so a gate is the prelude to a Scandinavian settlement, fairly recently unearthed. The dwelling sites, the granary, the general position demand no skilled knowledge to understand them. The settlement was discovered and dug up by unauthorized amateurs and almost led, I believe, to war between them and the scandalized professional archaeologists.

The return towards the Angler's Arms is a saunter, past the car park where no motorist is supposed to drive further east without a permit. Pause somewhere along the western shore for a final greeting to the scene, the uncompromising slopes of big Great Borne, of stern little Herdus, Red Pike, High Crag, Pillar and its classic Rock. Smile at a tiny island, the size of a cabin trunk, frequented by the odd cormorant. I enjoyed a lazy afternoon watching an infuriated angler in a boat catch nothing, while every ten minutes or so a cormorant dived in and emerged with a glistening snack.

From neighbouring Croasdale across to the hamlet of Ennerdale Bridge and on towards Kirkland rolls country that somehow belongs to yesterday. One place, at least, belongs to the day before that. I heard of it first from a Cumberland miner and his wife, dour but pleasant folk in their early forties. They were staying at an inn, and I shared the breakfast table with them. A mention of the supernatural happened to crop up, and the glance that passed between them made me say:

'But surely you don't believe in ghosts?'

The man said bluntly: 'Aye, we do. We've got to.'

I liked that. It had a savoury taste. I said: 'What about telling me all about it?'

The telling came in fits and starts, first the man, then the woman, back to the man, and it was jerky, a trifle ashamed, and utterly convincing. He said that in 1939 they had become engaged, and being keen fell-walkers, planned a Youth Hostel walking tour for that November. They were able to keep to their plan, despite the outbreak of war, because he and his girl were in reserved occupations. About four o'clock one misty November afternoon they came plodding into Ennerdale Bridge, their rucksacks heavy on their backs. They had booked in at the Ennerdale Youth Hostel for the night, but had no idea of its whereabouts. Some youngsters were scurrying out of the village school, and he called to them to tell him the way to the Hostel. To his surprise, they all looked scared and took to their heels.

'Fair fleyt (terrified) they were,' he said.

His wife nodded. 'But Tom managed to catch t'arm of a laal bairn.'

Tom repeated his question to the frightened little boy, and the child gabbled out some directions, snatched himself free, and bolted. It was curious and disconcerting. But they set off to follow his directions and after walking quite a while in the thickening twilight began to wonder whether he had either misled them or else they had turned into the wrong lane. Growing more and more doubtful and disheartened, seeing nothing but dim trees and shadowy fields, they were on the point of going back and asking for lodgings at the village inn, when they found themselves tramping past a long sandstone wall. This was cheering, for they knew that originally the Hostel had been a country house. They reached a gateway, and on one stoop they could make out the letters Y.H.A.

Behind, the grounds resembled a jungle, tangled trees and shrubs with a weedy drive groping through them. They emerged into a clearing to see in the dimness a big house. There was no sign of life. Dismayed, they walked up, knocked and knocked at the main door. Finally, half-uneasy, half-annoyed, Tom gave a shove, and the door opened silently upon a dark hall.

'Fair made me jump,' said Tom's wife.

A light glowed up in the gloom. It was a lamp held by a dwarf. They mentioned their names, and that they were booked here for the night, and in good broad Cumbrian he said: 'Aye, gaa yonder,' told them the numbers of their rooms, and pointed at a wide staircase.

They started up the stairs. It was so dark, Tom lit a match, and a cold draught blew from nowhere and put it out.

Mrs. Tom took up the story. She said that even before they reached the landing she had made up her mind not only to lock and bolt her bedroom that night, but to wedge something against the door; only to discover that the door had neither lock nor bolt.

They descended for the evening meal, and sat alone in a big, shadowy dining-room lit by two candles. The dwarf waited on them —appearing and disappearing at will, according to Mrs. Tom. Above the mantle-shelf hung a life-sized picture of a pretty young girl in bridal costume, her eyes wide open, but dead. They had been painted in such a way, there was no escape from them.

They whispered together, deciding that the only way to avoid these dreadful eyes was to go to bed soon with the hope of falling asleep quickly and forgetting the creepiness of Ennerdale Hall.

The dwarf gave each a candle-stick and a box of matches. They went up to the landing, kissed each other good-night, wished each other good-luck, and crossed to their rooms.

Mrs. Tom said: 'Ah dragged a laal dressin'-table over and pushed it against door.' After that she undressed quickly, got into bed, and blew out the candle.

At once the room was filled with a soft, silky hissing, the *frou-frou* of a wedding gown. For seconds she lay in this whispering darkness, too terrified to stir, to breathe. The dour breed of her forced her to her senses. She leapt out of bed, lit the candle, and the *frou-frou* died away. Knowing she dared not try to sleep, she perched on the edge of the bed, dragged the clothes around her shoulders, and simply waited for the hours to go by. The candle guttered out some while before dawn. She had been half-dozing. With the return of darkness the *frou-frou* was everywhere. In the end she dropped off from sheer exhaustion, awoke early, dressed in a rush, went across to Tom's room and tapped on the door.

It opened immediately, and he was standing there, dressed. It turned out that, like her, he had been kept awake by the ceaseless rustling of silk.

8   *Calder Hall atomic power station*

The two went down for an early breakfast, aching to get away from the place. The dead young bride in the picture watched them and watched them. They asked the dwarf about her, and he mumbled something about a lovely young bride dying in church.

At this point in the story it seemed to me that I was listening to some Victorian Gothic spine-chiller, delightful and ridiculous. Yet those two were matter-of-fact, grimly earnest. It suddenly occurred to me that the mother of the landlord here, an old lady in her eighties with a memory like a camera, might be able to provide some clue. I made an excuse to Tom and his wife, slipped through to the kitchen, mentioned Ennerdale Hall and the dead bride. The shrewd old eyes crinkled.

'Oo, aye. Happened when ah was a lass o'seventeen. Name of Elliot, hers was. Her feyther hed the big sandstone quarry at Eskett, an' built Ennerdale Hall.'

The lovely daughter grew up there, and became engaged to a young man from Buttermere. They were to be wed during the winter. The wedding day was bitterly cold and swirling with snow. The bride's friends and relations went along to the church, and then the bride and her father. But the groom failed to turn up, and at last the wedding party went back to the Hall, all except the bride, who refused to leave the church. She remained there all night, and next day the groom arrived. Great snow drifts the day before had stopped him from getting through. The two were married, but the night in the freezing church had done fatal damage. The bride was taken back home, to die a few days later from pneumonia.

Heartbroken, the parents had a portrait painted of their dead daughter in her bridal gown with her eyes open. It was hung above the mantelpiece, and for a few more sorrowing months they went on living in Ennerdale Hall. Unable to endure their grief there any longer, they let the place, with some of the furnishings, to the Y.H.A. So the true story held more romance and shadow than most Victorian fiction of that kind, and there is little more to add to it.

An acquaintance who digs deep and successfully in antique shops unearthed a framed photo taken about 1870. In the foreground was a typical Cumberland farmhouse with a stretch of lawn. Three women posed there, and a little girl lolled in front. At the back loomed a dark, steep, unforgiving fell. Could we identify this, the rest should be easy. After several expeditions we found that the dominating fell was Great Borne in Ennerdale. In the print it had been cleverly and subjectively tinted by rubbing in colour from the back. We picked out the farm, went there, and asked for the farmer. An elderly man, he came in from the fields, put on his spectacles, gave a chuckle of delight.

'Aye,' he said, ''tis ours. And yon laal lass in front was my granma.'

Somehow attracted by the severity of Great Borne, and by my description of a peculiar item near its summit, a large kind of wing chair made with sizeable slabs of stone taken from the surrounding clutter, my companion suggested a scramble up there one day.

We chose the wrong day. No sooner were we on the threshold of Ennerdale than the clouds dropped low, a wind whined mournfully, and rain swept the world. As an alternative, I suggested a hunt for Ennerdale Hall. The obliging landlady of the Shepherds Arms told us that the place had been pulled down. Apparently every hosteller who passed a night there had been kept awake by the *frou-frou* of the wedding gown. The Y.H.A. gave it up, and the hall was demolished, but the site remained, untouched, unvisited. She gave us clear directions, and in about 20 minutes we found the sandstone front wall of the grounds, and a gate stoop with the phantom lettering Y.H.A.

First, we went over to the enormous pinkish quarry behind. It was living, trucks moving here and there. We came back into the jungle of grounds, the foundations of the building and a few stone steps half-hidden by bushes and weeds. Branches creaked and scraped a little, rain pattered on the leaves, and their rustling in the dank gloom could easily have been taken for the *frou-frou* of silk. It was a relief to get away from its sorrow, and to see a promising gold band in the western sky. A hot spell might be on its way, and farmers would be juggling with the annual problem, whether to make hay first or to clip.

To the city dweller such alternatives are unlikely to touch the most impersonal fringe of thought. To the dalesman of the Lake District at this season they are hot-topical. Many farms are small, and until recently old ways prevailed, partly because of economics. Money invested in a baler and suchlike could be idle capital for 50 weeks of the year. No wonder visitors smiled at the antiquated yet charming methods of raking by hand, of sweeping with a contraption fixed to the front of the tractor, of forming footcocks and pikes, of tossing the hay upon wooden triangles. The very essence of summer and serenity dwelt in these sweet, slow ways of farming. One man who worked for us could slide his hayfork along the field until it had built up a load to appal a weight-lifter. With a thrust and a twist he would toss it lightly on to the truck.

Aye, sweet and slow they were, and because of their slowness, very vulnerable to our fickle weather. Nobody could get on with wet hay, and nobody could clip wet sheep. In a short, dry spell either sheep or hay had to wait, and July might be a drencher. But with modern machinery, at least the time taken up with hay is so reduced, a brief boon of sunshine may cover both jobs.

Towards the end of June some sheep-farm not far away is sure to be planning a gather for clipping. Find out the when and where, and if you are a strong walker, ask if you may join the gather. If not, you can dawdle up some minor trod and catch revealing glimpses from a modest viewpoint. This movement of men and dogs and the bringing down of the sheep has the ancient, almost New Testament significance of fishermen casting their nets. Join us, if you will, old Eb, young Derwent and myself at eight o'clock on a warm morning, the tops hazy with a mist that will melt as the sun gains power. We trudge up the rake, the steep ascent behind the farm, Gyp, Spy, Mac and Nell lolloping eagerly to heel. The first three are typical sheep-dogs, black, fluffy, white-throated and with other dabs of white here and there. Nell is more of a cur-dog, short-coated, mainly white, and resembling a large fox-terrier. A friend of mine had a cur-dog that at one bidding would set off on its own and return with the flock chivvied neatly down to the intake above the farmhouse.

We pass through the gate at the top of the rake. A wheatear clicks in protest and flicks its white skirt in dipping flight above some boulders. Presently, as we reach the first rocky terrace, there is a glimpse of two men waiting on a hummock towards the west. These are neighbours, for in this tall, wild and unfenced country, flocks tend to intermingle, and a joint gather saves a deal of time and labour. Soon we shall be seeing another pair of neighbours who will take care of the southern flank as we move forward on a wide sweep. The tactics of the affair suggest an advance of troops in the old days of the North-West Frontier, the main party choosing slightly lower ground in the middle, escorted by the protecting flankers.

Eb, Derwent and I fan out, cross a hollow of seeping sphagnum, pricked by sprigs of bog-myrtle with their young, heady scent. A yow and her lamb are sprawled on a small tilt of scree.

'E—Mac!' yells Derwent, 'there! E—Spy!'

Mac pelts off in a lefthand circuit, and Spy veers to the right. The gather is on and the work will be strenuous, for the yows and their lambs have had summery weeks of freedom and feel no urge to be down in the dale.

'E—Nell! E—Nell! Git awa'!'

Over there, just below a col where old heather squats thick and tangled, and small shattered crags form the sides of the col itself, a bunch of yows and their lambs are starting to drift northward. Nell's approach sends them scampering, all but one yow whose lamb seems a trifle lame. The rest pour through the col and vanish.

Eb grins genially. 'Fair booggers,' he says, and sends Gyp tearing westward around the col.

Meanwhile Nell has reached the limping lamb. Mother stamps her hoof and launches a butt. Nell, obviously amused, dips beneath it, avoids a second petulant butt, and gently noses the lamb towards the shallow dip below, the mother keeping pace, anxious and hostile. The mist is vanishing, and the western flank of Scafell emerges like some gigantic rocky walrus. Beyond the coast a carpet of silver and lilac is the Solway. Derwent brushes sweat from his nose, rests his crook against a boulder, lights a pipe of black twist. From the north starts a blurred chorus of shouting and shrill barking. Our neighbours have put up a fox. In a rufous flow it heads for the higher slopes, and the dogs, called back, return with a kind of gay, swaggering importance, mutely suggesting that they could have overtaken their quarry but for more urgent work.

In the centre a blaring caravan of yows and lambs grows longer and noisier. Then Eb stops by a yow standing alone, its manner strangely still and stupid. Getting closer, I can diagnose the sad trouble, that slight sway, the peculiar look in the left eye. The poor creature has a tumour on the brain. We shall have to get it down to the dale, where a man who is not a vet will perform the operation, making a hole in the soft centre at the top of the skull and removing the tumour, like a grisly bag of seeds, with a goose's feather.

By half-past ten we have reached the turn of the gather. The caravan in the middle pauses, blaring, whickering, snatching at tufts of fell herbage. The sun already has a bite, and we dab at our stickiness, thanking providence this is June and not July, when the midges can make the lives of man and beast a misery, and the clegs stab with the malice of poisoned darts.

Close by, a beck tumbles and fusses and froths down its channel of splintered granite. Spy and Mac sprawl flat in the water, mouths open to receive foam and bubbles. High overhead drifts a raven, uttering a lazy 'pronk—pronk'. I think in the heads of us men purrs an idea that we could do worse than idle here all day.

Our neighbours to the north are shouting and making gestures. We start on the return journey, the flankers sending in more stragglers to join the swelling convoy in the centre. Despite their vocal protests, these yows might well seem innocent to an inexperienced watcher. They drift and patter and jostle, occasionally jerking a butt at a dog that gets too close to their young; even so, they yet appear to be without guile. Approaching the upper intake at last, we halt while our distant neighbours make a wheeling movement, shooing forward the last detachment of stragglers. Just beyond the trod stretches a jungle of juicy young brackens, almond green, a seemingly enchanting tracery of fronds that would poison to death any unfortunate beast or sheep that ate many of them. As we are waiting, Derwent fills another pipe. He and Eb and I are watching a buzzard on the far side of the dale lazily avoiding the attacks of two crows. Luckily Gyp pays more attention to duty. A yow glances at the sanctuary of the brackens, gently nudges her lamb. Silent, unobtrusive as dissolving shadows, the pair disappear into the brackens and then stay dead still. There will be no movement to betray them, no slightest stir until we have passed on, out of sight. At least, that is the plan of guileless mamma. But Gyp slithers in among the fronds, and drives out the truants.

Derwent sucks in a pungent whiff of twist, and chuckles.

'Aye, fair booggers!'

The whickering procession moves on down through the upper gate of the intake. The dogs bark a little, sorting out the woolly congestion, Gyp leaping up on the wall as a sort of supervisor.

At the end of June, or in July, clipping is so characteristic of the Lakeland scene, to miss it would seem like visiting Kew without looking at the Gardens. On most farms the work is done by hand. Folk argue that clipping by machine may be all right for lordly Merinos and other breeds that have plentiful wool and run no risk of chilly summer nights on high. But the angular fell sheep are liable to be snicked by powered clippers, and they must be left with a 'vest' to protect them during July nights that can be quite cold.

Imagine a warm morning, the stackyard gates closed, and a bunch of confined yows waiting to be barbered, blaring to their lambs, penned in the intake. Eb and Derwent sit on low benches. George, a neighbour, is acting as usher, a dog at his heels. Eb grabs a yow, pulls her across his lap, makes a long cut across the belly wool. Derwent has tied his client's legs with oily rags, the better to control her. The quick, metallic snicking, the whicker and blare of the waiting yows, the wailing of the lambs, form a din that somehow gives no offence to the peaceful dale.

George is busy with many little duties. Like a dentist's receptionist he has to maintain the supply of reluctant clients. Every so often he carries a bundle of fleeces to the upper floor of the barn. In between whiles is the important business of smitting the clipped sheep, in other words, staining the yows with their flock-mark. He does it with a stick dipped into a pot of dye, red in this case. Every flock has its registered mark in the Shepherd's Guide. They used to 'rit' the ears as well, but these days ear-tags are fixed on instead.

Naked, almost self-conscious, bunches of clipped yows are returned to the intake. Bewildered lambs, failing at first to identify their mothers, fill the air with their falsetto implorings. Three innocent walkers, two kindly women and a man, town dwellers, have stopped by the edge of the road and are staring at the scene. They wince at a yow with a ghastly red smear across her loins, jump to an entirely wrong conclusion, and glare at Derwent for being seemingly careless and cruel. Giggling within, he stares back coldly. Eb chuckles, shakes his head at the strangers, and jerks his thumb towards the smit pot.

The day grows warmer, a silver haze quivering about the fells. Bees are droning among the tops of the sycamores. Across the way a beck sliding whitely down through the shadow of a deep ghyll makes me wish I were over there instead of over here. Behind the intake wall whin pods are popping under the heat of the sun. Eb flicks sweat from his eyelids and reckons the day is a fair capper. Aye.

Over a period of hours, the clipping rate works out at six and a half minutes per yow. To townsfolk the job might connote monotony, but it involves a deal of skill, and that lessens the threat of boredom. Besides, extra help is available by reason of boon days, neighbours lending a hand to one another, and a man can chat while he clips, and rich gossip makes time fly past.

The greasy fleeces are beginning to pile up in the barn, where they will lose a little weight before they change hands. Dinner time passes, drowsy afternoon wears on, and the haze on the fells gives way to a clearer light, so that cracks in the rocks are etched sharply. The work continues until the valley floor stirs with shadows, shadows that flow up and up the fell-breasts like some swelling, copper sea. The clipped and their young are drifting up the fell beyond the intake, their chorus thinning away to a few minor blares and whickerings that somehow get absorbed into the green evening quietude.

Eb rises, stretches himself, looks at Derwent. 'Hoo's fettle (how are you feeling)?'

Derwent wipes his hand across his mouth. 'Laike a quart.'

Some of us were having a crack about sheep in the local when a visitor said: 'It must be very convenient to own a hill flock. I mean, apart from lambing and dipping and shearing, you don't have to bother about them at all, do you?'

The explosion of laughter surprised him, for he was an intelligent man. He looked from one to another, and went on: 'Have I said something wrong?'

An elderly shepherd started the ball rolling. He talked of tormentil, the tiny golden flower known to the botanists as *potentilla erecta*. By trillions of trillions it scatters its innocence along the banks of the dale roads and the lower skirts of the fells. It looks like a flower out of a fairy story for very young children. Inevitably sheep pick up some of it while browsing; if they then rest in shadow, no malignance affects them; if they go on wandering in the sunshine, the poison of *tormentil* sets up a soreness of the muzzle, inflamed eyes, and sometimes an actual decay of the ears.

'Aye,' said a thin, dour farmer. 'And hesta (have you) nivver heard o' liver-fluke? 'tis picked oop fra some o' them wet spots.'

'Or maggot-fly?' said someone else.

We admitted that things were easier than they used to be; that dipping was a straight-forward business compared with the old days, when each and every sheep had to be smeared all over by hand with a special ointment; even so, many a poor yow died horribly, the fly laying in the fleece eggs that hatched out as maggots, these eating the animal alive so that it was reduced to wool and bone, and a man might pick it up between fore-finger and thumb.

The visitor's features wrinkled into a shocked grimace. For the first time he was appreciating that there is a reverse side to the charming, idyllic picture of the peaceful sheep grazing on the picturesque hillside. He heard of cragfast sheep, of sheep that fell into becks and gutters and because of the weight of water in their fleece and the soggy moss and slippery banks, died there in misery. I told him of a macabre incident I met on a moorland track, the day dreary and colourless; to my left was a mossy swamp, and something protruding looked too queer to be a tiny hummock. It turned out to be the heavily horned head of a fine Swaledale tup. The rest of its body remained beneath the mire, where it had died standing.

Taking compassion on the visitor, we switched over to more flippant matters.

CHAPTER FIVE

July

I like to think that our fore-elders had a natural flair for euphony. How, otherwise, could they have fashioned the names of the three sisters, Loweswater, Crummock, and Buttermere? Loweswater suggests a wide-eyed, innocent child resting but watching in a green cot. The slopes around her are gentle, and her reflections of them in early morning make it worthwhile getting up, if not with the lark, at least well before breakfast. Later on there may be the handicap of many admirers. Surely earliness in summer is no great anguish? and the young hours, like Loweswater, have an innocence. Quietude, the thin, pearly light, rabbits and pigeons unafraid and ravaging tender shoots, these things cast a spell of a picture in a fairy story—except, of course, on the outraged farmer. Townsfolk staying in the more secluded parts of Lakeland must accept that, in the phase following dawn, Nature can be charming and infuriating in the same breath. An inquisitive magpie seeing itself in a window desecrates the hush by bashing its beak against the glass. More than once a green woodpecker has roused me from sleep with its rowdy cackle, and for seconds my thoughts have been murderous, until the cackle has so resembled the laughter of a fat old lady in the village bus, I have finished up by laughing myself.

Earliness does indeed reveal a different world, when Nature seems to assume an intimate, unguarded mood. But she still provides a lot, should you come to Loweswater later in the day. Over there, and—to use a peculiar expression about a fell—never unbending, Mellbreak stands stiff on duty, steep, harsh, a trifle frightening to a plainsman. Above Mellbreak circle a pair of buzzards. An optimist could mistake them for golden eagles. In actual wing span, a big hen buzzard would be comparable with an immature eagle, for I have seen buzzards with a span of over five feet, and these days young eagles are immigrating across the Solway, an overspill from Galloway where their elders insist on ample space.

The buzzards above Mellbreak have spotted a dead sheep, a Herdwick yow perhaps slain by liver-fluke. They are preparing to swoop down and feed, a sight as characteristic of the area as is an accident on the M.1. The slow beat of their rather broad wings decreases, and they perch by the carcase. Being tidy eaters, they peck away the wool and the hair beneath before attempting to tear at the flesh. They prefer carrion to live meat, and that is fortunate for the fell-farmer. Buzzards that turned to attacking lambs would be a major menace.

High up, a big bird with slightly retracted wings, and not unlike a buzzard in silhouette, is dipping and stalling. A deep 'pronk, pronk' drifts across the sky, the note of a raven preparing to join the feast. A messy eater, he will dig in his powerful beak, rending and snatching and guzzling and getting his eyes smeared with fat and offal. Before his final dive to the ground, he twists himself into a sort of victory roll.

The buzzards consider his approach with what may be disgust, or annoyance, or both. But there will be no fighting over the spoils. There is more than enough for the moment.

These scavengers, together with the fox, are invaluable to the fell country. In hard winters, such as the protracted snows of 1947, flocks are bound to suffer heavy losses. They take refuge in sheltered spots, and where there is sanctuary from the wind, there the snow lies deeper and deeper. Beneath it some sheep can survive up to a month, nibbling the sod and one another's fleece. Inevitably many starve to death. All over the fells, a long, Arctic spell will kill thousands. But for the scavengers, the arrival of the thaw would degrade the uplands into a stinking charnel house. Even so, there are times when a walker will grab his nose and run fast. Such odours prompt the philosophic to wonder what London and other cities must have been like in the old days, when the only dustmen were the kite, protected by law—and probably the buzzard.

The vale of Lorton, beyond Loweswater, sounds like the title of some charming old song. Lorton, too, has innocence, because of its mild slope and what Victorian writers used to describe as open countenance. You may care to watch a hound-trail here. To the dalesman, a trail is as vital as cricket to a worshipper of Lords or the Oval. Possibly millions of southerners have never heard of trailing. In that case, may I say a little about the background before you watch the event?

The hounds are slender, wiry, wasp-waisted. They look as if they have been trained for ballet-dancing, foxhounds with a difference. It used to be said that owners of whippets fed them on steak, and their wives and children on bread and marge. I would not offer this comparison concerning trail-hounds and their owners, but certainly the diet is rich. The recipe of the special dish of cock-loaf, for instance, involves flour, sherry, port, raisins, eggs, cooked as a pudding, then cut into slices and toasted. This may be washed down with butter-milk. I know not whether the dish would make me sick, or go to sleep in front of the fire. To the trail-hound it gives speed and stamina.

Football has its F.A., and hound-trailing its H.T.A. Trails are run during seven or eight months of the year, in suitable areas all over Lakeland and its fringes. For dogs the trail is about ten miles, and for puppies half the distance. Almost always the layers of the trail are young men with fine lungs and a springy step. Each carries a sack and a bottle of aniseed and paraffin. The demand for aniseed persuaded cottagers to grow it in their gardens, and I know places where it straggles down road-banks.

The trail runs roughly in a circuit, starting and finishing at some valley field, and the trail-layers begin at the centre, each working backwards towards the valley.

Join the crowd pouring into the field. Vans are arriving, and jacketed hounds are jumping out, and being put on leashes and 'walked' gently. Over by that wall rises a chorus from the line of bookies' stands; potential backers are studying the boards and telling one another what is bound to win, and privately wondering whether they might be wrong. Roamingdale, the favourite, has the discouragingly short odds of seven to two on. Next is Stardust at five to one. The massed voices of the punters grow louder, and with the yowling and yapping of the trail-hounds, the general noise suggests a cantata of hope, anxiety, and desire especially devised as a prelude to hound-trailing.

A man with a limp and strong lungs bellows something indistinguishable. Owners, or slippers set off for the start-line, and begin to form up; the behaviour of the trail-hounds with them varies from wild excitement to a deedy calmness. Facing them, a 100 yards in front, runs a wall. Nearer, on the flank, waits the starter with a white handkerchief. From hound to hound walks an official who makes a special mark on the competitors, with the hope of checking villainy, in that a scoundrel hidden half-way round the course might pick up his hound and substitute a fresh one.

Howling and yapping rise to a climax. Some of the hounds are straining at the leash and trembling violently. Then a man with a sack scrambles over the wall, runs forward a few paces, and as the handkerchief drops, snatches up his sack. With a concerted yowl the unleashed hounds pour past him, a rippling flow of white and tan, lemon and tan, black and white, leap the wall with the effortless ease of rising birds, fling themselves up a trod flanked by brackens, reach a damp spot where they spatter through sphagnum moss, swerve along a stony tilt. Though still fairly compact, there is 50 yards between the leader and the tail-end. Seconds later those dots are bobbing out of sight beyond the lip of the fell, and the high pitch of excitement subsides to an undertone.

Bookies are still offering the odds. A man with a walkie-talkie may be up there among the crumpled heights, sending back news of the hounds. Within minutes heads swing westward, binoculars are jammed to eyes, and somebody screeches and points. There they are, pouring along a high trod on the fell-breast opposite, splashing among slurry, next across a steep pitch of scree, vanishing for moments among a clutter of large boulders.

The sharp-eyed are yelling out names. 'Roamingdale! Stardust! Misty Lad!'

One hound, no more than a fleck of paleness to my straining sight, has somehow run off the scent, scampered further up the fell, and realizing its mistake, descends a diagonal ledge to find its way barred by a drop of perhaps 12 feet. With the velvety spring of a panther it gains some tufty ground below and joins the rest of the careering hounds. They are about half-way around the trail, having covered five steep and stony miles in 15 minutes. What after this, I wonder, would be the condition of a southern foxhound?

Again they are out of sight, lost in a hollow where whins grow thick; may the pads of all escape the vicious prickliness. A thorn in the paw of a game trail-hound is a sad business. Worse can be the effect of extra sharp scree. I have seen hounds limping in with bloody feet, and the owner of one, a girl, running to gather him with tears rolling down her cheeks.

Five more minutes pass, and by now, we know, they are crossing the valley and scampering up the run of fell on our side. At any minute a keen-eyed dalesman will shout his head off and point triumphantly.

Up there, at the base of a buttress, a few yows are browsing on the bents. To me, at that distance, they might be greyish-brown mice. There is movement among them, a sudden scuttling as they take flight over a hummock. Something has scared them, and ten to one it will be the trail-hounds.

An elderly shepherd with a face of lined leather and the voice of a hunting horn swings up a pointing hand. 'Yonder they gaa! Roamin'dale! Roamin'dale! Misty Lad!'

How in the name of miracles he can distinguish them at that range is beyond my guessing. His father must have been a peregrine. More and more join in, waving and yelling, and at the top of a green trod flanked by brackens the little descending blobs are growing bigger. The men around me become pleasantly mad, waving, bawling, imploring. Owners and slippers whistle, shriek the names of their hounds. Cumbrians are dour, aye, but moments such as this are stronger than old ale.

Roamingdale is leading by a couple of yards, flowing between the brackens towards the wall. Stardust leads Misty Lad by a foot or two. Their owners are jumping up and down, holding out tins with savoury tidbits, bawling, crooning, praying with ecstatic incoherence. Roamingdale clears the wall, approaches the finishing line at a pelting lollop, snatches at his meaty reward. Stardust gobbles, and wriggles and waggles under his owner's acclaiming hands. Another hound-trail is over, and somebody has lost money, and somebody has won a little.

Where sport and money mix, a pinch of villainy is bound to accompany the blend. With all the will in the world, no committee can eliminate it entirely. The main run of a trail of such length cannot be kept exclusively secret. Think of a villain hiding in some gully or heathery hollow on high, waiting to toss to the leading favourite a juicy bit of roast mutton. The proudest hound would be willing to come in last on such a meal. There is the man who crouches by the loop of a trail, snatches up his hound, and takes it straight across to the final bend. I recall a case of this years ago when the scoundrel was downright stupid. He cut out so much of the trail, his hound's speed worked out at about 60 miles per hour.

More subtle was the affair of a trail held fairly near the coast. In the morning a bookie's clerk approached a friend of mine and told him not to back the favourite. So we both put our money on the next best, and wondered what jiggery pokery might be in the air. A good deal of the trail was on comparatively flat land, the last half mile or so through a series of fields, spectators lining both sides. Presently, to the accompaniment of yelling, the favourite appeared, leading by at least 10 yards.

My friend grunted, and said: 'Yon clerk knew nowt, the gowk!'

Those were my sentiments, too. We had been led up the garden path. And yet, with 600 yards to go, the favourite slackened, almost imperceptibly, but enough for the second best to pass him with five yards to spare. My bewildered friend and I collected our unhallowed gains and wondered how on earth the trick could have been performed under the noses of the crowd. It took me a year to excavate the answer. A moment before the start, the owner had slid a rubber band over the toe of the favourite. After miles of speed the toe began to swell a little, and the elastic naturally grew tighter. The owner, of course, had backed the second best.

July

If I am accused of spending too many words on hound-trailing, my answer can only be this, that hound-trailing *is* the Lake District, much more than gift shops and such-like. It has a physical beauty about it, costs nothing to watch, and takes place through the bulk of the year.

As a change from staring at the distant, the visitor who drives slowly or walks gently about the vale of Lorton may enjoy close-up aspects of another kind. Like other dales, it has what can be described as wall-furniture, hogg-holes, the economical alternative to a gate, where sheep may pass through, with a slab lying handy to block the gap. There are grikes, V-shaped openings in the tops of walls, with a stone below to serve as a step up to the V. There are several varieties of cam stones, parapets to strengthen the rim of the wall. I wish some photographer would bring out a book on our walls, with colour pictures of the ferns and mosses and lichens that colonize them. Again, this is essentially the Lake District.

How many folk, in passing, pay much heed to the small fields themselves? In the summer, some may be under pasture, grazed by beasts, or sheep, and a few under crops. A very wet depression will harbour a few seeves. Pick one, skin it carefully, and notice how the pith serves ideally as the core of a tallow dip. This is a close link with the fairly recent past. The nettles that ought not to be there make a most palatable nettle pudding if cut young and cooked with barley. The result is better than spinach.

Under these fields hides something that can be queerly interesting. The term field drainage hardly suggests a subject holding any fascination. Although vital to farming, the modern form of it, relying on drain-pipes, offers scant romance. But here and there these small fields, with their ancient, appealing names, Tarn Ling, Tup Close, Rake Ring, Many Pieces, retain their original drainage, and that is enough to make a boy babble with delight and a grown man say to his wife: 'Just a few minutes, m'dear. It's really worth looking at.'

The first time I encountered this medieval work was in a swampy pasture near our farmhouse. We dug down between two and three feet to find out why it was getting wetter and wetter. There, instead

of pipes, were small chunks of granite, laid in a double course as a channel about five inches wide, and roofed by single chunks of granite, forming a primitive gutter. To enable the water to drain through into the gutter brackens had been packed between the granite chunks. It seemed a shame to disturb this ancient skill, but many of the chunks had been disrupted by the roots of a great ash tree, that long-range seeker after water, and the brackens were rotten; so we were forced to switch over to banal, reliable drainpipes.

During our digging we unearthed several old clay tobacco pipes and a ring green with eld. This had faint, raised markings, and since Lakeland has in its soil an astonishing quantity of items left behind by the Roman occupation, our hopes rose high. Somebody suggested that it might belong to the chin-strap of a Roman legionary, the markings being the number of his Legion. An amateur archaeologist offered to show it to his president. A week later we received the verdict. The ring was off a whipstock made in Birmingham about 80 years back. But we had enjoyed our ration of conjecture.

In the convulsive past here, Nature must have been thinking in three's, for the three lakes have three passes as neighbours. An almost private way to Whinlatter is to turn down by a signpost marked Hope Beck. The lonnin then takes charge of you in a meandering and confidential mood and climbs to the open fell. Until recently, the surface was dubious. Now it has a hard skin, and its passage over the fell begets buoyancy. Nobody in haste should drive up here. In greyness or brilliance, the road invites idling, and idling, I feel, is a first cousin to courtesy. Your charioteer in a ruthless hurry juggles with bad manners and death. There is no cure for the second state, but the first can be modified by the right kind of rebuke. A friend of mine brought me back from Wasdale Show at excessive speed, driving on the tail of a local car and hooting impatiently. That narrow section of the road precluded any chance of passing. Then my embarrassment was changed to delight. The dalesman driver in front waved us down, stopped his car, walked back to ours. Much too wise to swear, he smiled at my silly friend, raised his hat, and said:

'My car's gey old and slow. Yours is new and fast. Directly there's a chance, I'll make room. Thank you.'

He smiled again, raised his hat once more. My friend went scarlet.

This Hope Beck lonnin brings you out well up Whinlatter, with its displays of stone and heather and trees. The crowded timber can prove awkward in spring and early summer and late autumn, for it holds the summit of the pass in almost perpetual shadow. Light snow may have melted away under the sun and invited you to be up and over. Near the top the clear road abruptly assumes deep whiteness.

Sister Crummock invites you towards the second pass, Newlands. I would give a lot for a glimpse of the journey here as it was a 100 years ago. In these years of grace and petrol a briskness of traffic is inevitable. The big fells on the far side of the lake, Red Pike, High Stile and the lesser giants wall off Ennerdale. Along their stony and wind-swept spines walking is both a challenge and a taste of immortality. Fine weather helps, though rain and mist will provide fascination as well as fear. In those conditions, a compass and a map ought to be useful. I use the verb 'ought', because the truth is sometimes otherwise. Never can I forget a woman doctor, young and delightful as a spring flower, who fell in love with the high hills. With no sense of direction, she went out on her own and was badly lost. The exhausting experience failed to deter her, and so I persuaded her to promise to take no more solitary walks until she had bought a map and compass. She did so, and came up Buttermere Red Pike with me out of Ennerdale. As we reached the summit, thick mist closed down.

'Now's your chance,' I said. 'Where's Eskdale?'

She pointed through the murk in the direction of Crummock. I shook my head, and suggested she should get out her map and compass.

Her smile was like moonlight on water. 'Of course I will. But I haven't the slightest idea how to use them.'

One kind of weather I abominate and dread on the fells, a thunder storm. To be by Crummock and watch lightning play over Red Pike is alarming. To be on Red Pike itself, in the middle of the display, is terrifying to my craven and sinful spirit. Three of us walking there on a sultry afternoon saw purple thickness brewing over Gable. Blue flashes and flickers lit up the murk. I tried to calculate the course the storm would travel, and decided that if we veered half left, in the direction of Wharnscale Bottom, we might avoid the worst. So we moved very fast until the tail-end of a hail bombardment drove us to cover beneath some crags.

While we crouched, I recalled the weird tricks of electrical storms. Leading some friends down Stirrup Crag, on Yewbarrow, a storm in the offing, I had turned to beckon, and seen the hair of one girl stand straight on end. The hair of the other girl followed suit. A yelp from the man heralded a similar performance by his shorter crop. Very dry hail was falling. Then my balding pate prickled, and my few hairs stood erect.

This storm on Red Pike soon passed over, and we left the shelter of the crags and aimed for High Stile. The sun was out somewhere, for in the distance, by the side of an ebony peak, jutted another of gold. I secretly prayed that there might be no more lightning.

The most unnerving ordeal I have met on high was to go blind. Against my will, because of a damaged kneecap, I agreed to escort friends to Windy Gap. There I proposed to turn back, but they egged me on to ascend Pillar. It struck me that the best way of tackling the steepish ascent would be to rush it. By working up a momentum, I thought, there would be less strain on the knee. So I told them to come on in their own time, and dashed off ahead for the summit.

Half-way up my eyes failed, and I could only just distinguish between darkness and light. Appalled, I closed my lids, waited a little while, opened them. I could see nothing. Groping my way on with my hands, and by the feel of the fell under my boots, I kept assuring myself that all would be well soon. 'Don't tell the others, don't tell the others.' The words kept repeating themselves in my head. I found the cairn with my hands, sat on the flattened edge of it, my lids shut tightly. The longer I waited, the more was I afraid to open them. Soon the voices of my friends were drawing near. I had to open one lid a millimetre, and saw stone, and bents, and the sky. If I failed to mutter: 'Praise God from whom all blessings flow,' at any rate the thanks were in me.

July

For a year I hugged the nasty secret, wondering, on solitary walks, if I might be suddenly blinded again. In the end, out on the fells with two medical friends, I stammered my story. They were sensible enough to laugh, and explained that in my dash up Pillar I had drained the blood out of my head to help my legs, and deprived the optic nerves. I wished I had made my confession a year earlier.

Back on High Stile, the airy brightness again faded, and Gable vanished under a swaying pall torn by zigzag flashes. This second storm appeared to be launching itself straight at us. By unspoken agreement we ran and slid and stumbled down the fellside towards the Ennerdale plantations. To court trees in a storm might seem crazy, but we believed that in this direction lay escape from its orbit. We guessed aright; compared with those hostile flashes, stumbling over roots, bumping our elbows against rough bark, and other minor sufferings were quite enjoyable.

Before Newlands pass opens its seductive lips to the north, the south presents another excitement, Sour Milk Ghyll bubbling and creaming down the fell-breast. In truly wet weather its torrents deserve more than a glance and a few words of praise. To the dry-mouthed fell-walker it must appear as the monarch of all thirst-quenchers. There are curious arguments about the drinking of beck-water. First, there are Spartans who oppose it on principle. The more you drink, the more you thirst, they say, and advise total abstinence. As a tyro, out with the Eskdale and Ennerdale pack, I sat on a boulder with the late Will Porter, huntsman and Master for half a century. A beck frothed nearby, and I went for a mouthful. He rebuked me. His advice was, a flask of tea at four, and nothing else. That way, he insisted, you felt much fitter during a long day on the fells. It took me months before I trained myself to live up to his advice, and found it invaluable.

As for the purity of the water itself, a beck descending steeply, continually splashing among rocks, and creating oxygenation, provides water probably safer than any that came out of a pipe. As in everything else, common sense counts most. Anybody who fails to look well upstream for the presence of a dead sheep is being foolish.

Buttermere, the third of the glimmering trinity, is a benevolent prelude to the harsh ascent of Honister Pass. The green slate crags on the summit have seen generations of quarrymen. The old, disused cable track, called the Drumhouse, coaxes even the lazy into tentative walking. They leave their cars somewhere, and potter up and up, and some of the most determined get over Brandreth and Green Gable to Gable herself. The Puritans of fell-walking sniff at such performances. To tackle Gable from the summit of Honister, they claim, is cheating, and to walk up there in town clothes an insult to the fells. With these sentiments I entirely disagree. Good luck to the novice who steps out of a car and experiments, perhaps rather diffidently at first, in the use of his feet.

As for clothes, this aspect involves a vein of inverted snobbery. One of the toughest walkers I ever knew always wore a blue serge suit, a bowler hat, and a heavy gold watch chain. In the gully of Esk Hause, on a hot day, I met two pretty girls clad in summer frocks and airy-fairy shoes. Three mountaineering tigers, plodding up the weariness of Gavel Neese, rested by a boulder and heard movement below. There came up past them, moving fast, a man in a black jacket and waistcoat, striped trousers, a black Homburg, and carrying a black brief-case. He said 'Good-morning, gentlemen,' and disappeared above, around a bend in the steep and scree-hidden trod.

Clothes make neither the man nor the climber. I grant that those girls should have worn stout shoes or boots, that the blue-serge addict and the man with the black case ought to have carried a good mac, or waterproof trousers, or both. I hold no brief for the folk who go aloft without full provision for a dangerous change of weather. But a blue serge suit, *per se*, has as much right to the fells as an anorak with a hood. In fact, I believe I prefer it, as a rarity, like a gentian rather than a golden star of *tormentil*. I have not seen a blue serge suit for years.

CHAPTER SIX

August

Possibly the best way to enjoy the comfort of bed is after a day of hard manual labour. Without any disrespect, I suggest that the best way to enjoy Grasmere is to go there via Eskdale, preferably by the hill known as Red Bank. The first time I drove down this hill the surface was so rutted and loose, my companion shut his eyes, and by the quivering movements of his lips, seemed to be mumbling prayers of supplication. In so doing he missed a deal of excitement and a revelation of beautiful scenery framed by splendid trees.

The contrast between the rigours of Eskdale and the graces of Grasmere is quite extraordinary. The one has aloofness, a fine austerity; it reminds man that he is there only on sufferance; the other extends the bosomy invitation of a well-dressed, lovely woman. It also has gift shops, weaving, and the notable sports. Here is Wordsworth country, and the likely explanation of how and why his later work lost its genius. I forget who compared his second phase with the blarings of an old yow. The comparison smacks painfully of truth.

No doubt his sympathy with the French revolutionaries was merely academic, unlike his secret affair with the young French girl. Had the truth come out in his youthful days, instead of emerging after his respectable death, he might have been a better poet. He might have brought her back and settled down with her in the fine solitude of the Duddon valley, the sanctuary of his boyhood holidays. Not for him, then, the social round of polished Grasmere, the polite tittle-tattle, the post-office income and the portentous reputation. The continued struggle, hard living, the inspired realities of Dunnerdale, these things would have sharpened his mind and his pen. Today's world may say: 'What of it? Who was he, anyway?'

Grasmere, Rydal, Dove Cottage, these have been linked with Wordsworthian literature almost *ad nauseam*. Yet I imagine that in recent years they have faded, not in themselves, but in what they used to conjure up for awed and worshipping pilgrims. The lamps of the shrine burn dim, as do those of another giant who lived not far away, Ruskin.

Once upon a time Coniston meant Ruskin, and Ruskin meant Coniston. People stayed in the village for the honour of seeing him pass by. A friendly, comfortable little village, Coniston. At one period quite half its working inhabitants must have made a living out of the quarries that scar Coniston Old Man. The name sounds a little impertinent for a dignified fell. Faulty spelling is to blame. The original Scandinavian title, Alt Maen, tall hill, ought to be given back to it. The quarries themselves escaped Ruskin's criticism. They provided exquisite roofing. He used it for Brantwood, the house he bought from the Lynton family. In the main, the alterations he made there were horrible. But those who drive along the north bank of the lake, a progress of leafy charm, need not look too closely.

Had Ruskin's parents worshipped him less, his marriage could have been happy. Poor Effie! if she is to be blamed at all for failing to hold him for better or worse, her failure lies in not slapping his face. According to all evidence, she did her excellent best as a wife, except to make him realize his limitations. A man who dared to pronounce not mere opinions but god-like edicts on such matters as scenery needed a good, hard slap.

Oddly, he seems to have been much more modest about his architectural drawings. Many are housed in the tiny museum at the back of Coniston village. Nobody could have blamed Ruskin for being proud of these elegant skills. Years ago I spent an afternoon envying the hand and the eye that could produce such work. Admission to the museum was, and still is, I suppose, via a turnstile operated by a penny in the slot. Earlier that afternoon it had presented an alarming problem. Our party consisted of myself and two ladies, one slim, the other not so slim.

I dropped in the first penny, and the slim lady passed through with an effortless *clink*. I dropped in the second. The not so slim lady pressed forward. The turnstile moved round half its allotted span, and then stuck, trapping her neatly. She used her weight, to no avail. She pushed, and I pushed, and the slim one pulled, to no avail. She beat at the curve of iron and cried: 'I will! I must!' to no avail. The great Ruskin himself might have been disconcerted.

After breathless and exhausting minutes we held a conference. There was no attendant. What sort of an expert did we need? A fireman? Would there be one in tiny Coniston? What about a blacksmith? H'm. Such craftsmen were growing scarce. There was just a chance we might find a smith in the place. Or perhaps a policeman?

'You stay with her,' said the slim lady, 'and I'll go out and see what I can find.'

She hurried around the circuit and came out via the exit turnstile. The sound of it stimulated my sluggard brain. Experimentally I dropped in another penny. With a *clink* the not so slim lady passed through, a free woman. I dared not hint that perhaps the price of admission depended on quantity.

South of Coniston and west of Coniston spreads a wealth of innocent temptation, some of it not strictly a part of the Lake District. To be so near and to miss it is almost sinful. Broughton-in-Furness points the way. Broughton can have changed little in a century. There the wicked young Branwell Brontë took his first job as tutor to a small boy named Postlethwaite. He was thrown out for making love to the little boy's mother. The little boy's son was living in Broughton until a few years ago, and at lunch with me would talk willingly on any subject except Branwell.

Kirkby-in-Furness sleeps by the shore and the sea-washed Cumberland turf, and out of it there leaps up to the moors an exultant road, nearly swamped in season by the pressing oceans of heather. Far below shine the waters of Morecambe Bay, and these airy, purple, sea-girt uplands are the introduction to Ulverston, one of those small North Lancashire towns that can call themselves blessed. Lord

Birkett was born and bred in Ulverston. That would help to account for his charm and courtesy and wise discernment. A little while after the Second World War two men I knew drove up to Birker Moor on their way to a holiday at Wasdale Head. The gate on the fell-road was about to be closed by an elderly man wearing an ancient mac. He held it open for them and they tipped him three-pence. Then they noticed that he was walking back to a quiet but distinguished car. They saw it next at Wasdale Head, parked outside the hotel. They described it to the barman and asked if he knew the owner.

'Aye. Lord Birkett.'

In the middle of Ulverston a mill of grey stone flanks the narrow approach to the car park. Carved in the stone, close to the doorway, are the heads of a schoolgirl, a middle-aged woman, and a grand-mother. I ventured to ask about them, and the mill-owner said they had been shaped by his father in spare time, and then showed me other carvings, with a leisurely friendliness that warmed the heart. Such is Ulverston.

A mile or two beyond, in utter peace, stands the house of Swarth-moor, the Mecca of Quakers. Here George Fox was received and tended in honour. The ex-headmaster of the Friends' School at Wigton guided me over the place, and its serenity came around us like some sanctified cloak. Everything seemed quietly and humanly lovable, even the old Quaker bonnets he showed me, devotions of fine grey silk. The Meeting House, built by George Fox, is between Swarthmoor and Ulverston. This, too, has the simplicity and peace created by the Friends. By reason of hinged panels, space for few can be altered in a minute to space for many.

Geographically we are on the inviting, slippery slope. After all, from Ulverston to Cartmel and Grange the journey is a mere frac-tional sally by car. Cartmel Priory alone deserves the extra miles. The village rivals the spoiled darlings of the Cotswolds, with the added bewitchment that should it be wet, you may have the flowers and the silvery stone and the lacework of becks to yourself. Over the fell lies Grange. A poor, misguided southerner said to me:

'I suppose Grange is like Blackpool?'

I showed him a coloured photo. He stared and stared, and said: 'Isn't there any road along by the promenade?'

'There isn't.'

He considered the tilted sweep of parks, the flowery promenade, the lilac-blue, distant shores, east and south and west, so that his mind's eye grew happily lost.

'As the crow or any sensible bird flies,' I said, 'it's on the very doorstep of the Lake District.'

Now he is retired, and settled there. He appreciates the story of a Lancashire Darby and Joan, sitting in front of the fire on a cold winter's evening in Preston.

Darby said: 'Thou's quiet.'

'Aye. Ah's thinking.'

'What's thou thinking aboot?'

'Us.'

'And what's thou thinking aboot us?'

Joan said slowly: 'Ah's thinking that if owt happens to either of us, ah's goin' to live at Grange.'

North Lancashire has brought us from Broughton, and must take us back there and on to Langdale in Westmorland. Past the New Dungeon Ghyll and the Old, a lesser road links up with Little Langdale. From a point near Fellfoot the view of the Langdale Pikes is startling. They look nobly grim, merciless. From the top of Bowfell they are harmless mounds, and that seems a shame. But far be it from me to criticize Nature's business. We even accuse her of cruelty, of redness in tooth and claw, and unless we are vegetarians we have scant right to make accusations. Appetite deadens our sense of justice, and sentiment makes things worse. I am reminded of an episode at Little Langdale Tarn, on the right of the road between Fellfoot and Skelwith Bridge.

Friends of mine have a house opposite this tarn. One bright, bitter-hard morning the good lady got up and glanced out of her bedroom window. The ground was blanched and glistening with frost, the tarn burnished steel. Something moved in the centre of the steel, something that fluttered a little but remained in position. It was a pair of whooper swans. They must have settled on a pool of open water at dusk and now they were gripped tight. Something else was moving, on the bank, rufous and stealthy. A fox had seized its chance.

There was no gun in the house, and no time to throw on some clothes and rush across to the tarn and scare the fox away. Vainly she shouted, and waved her arms, while the fox began to prowl over the ice. Her shouts aroused her husband. He reckoned the swans would put up a vigorous fight, but being fixed, they were bound to lose. In open water they would have drowned Reynard with fierce efficiency.

The nearer Reynard got, the more violent grew their fluttering. The good lady was close to tears. As her eyes winced with dread at what she expected, the sudden, final spring, there was a whirlwind of fluttering and the swans broke free. They flew in the direction of the house, whooping shrilly, and as they passed above she could see their naked pink breasts where the ice had ripped off the feathers.

Wrynose pass, rising out of Little Langdale, could tell a most unfair story of broken romance. The sufferer was a shepherd we all liked and admired, quiet, modest, good at his job and a prodigious walker. His work was at the head of Eskdale, and he fell in love with a lass of Little Langdale. He had no car. So two or three times a week, after tidying up, he walked over Hardknot and Wrynose. Speaking statistically, he started at an altitude of about 300, ascended to 1,290, descended to 750, ascended to 1,280, and descended to 300. The mileage for the single journey is about nine. Statistics, I know, have little influence on the course of love. I can recall my own first and far-distant love affair when between my house and hers my shoes never touched the pavement. But even Eros must have been impressed by that shepherd's performance. I recall mentioning it to a motorist, who raised his brows and said:

'That accounts for it. I was driving over Hardknot the other evening, and a pedestrian passed me.'

The words are his, and he looked an honest man. If ever a shepherd deserved his Amaryllis, Tom did. But after six months of Olympic wooing he was turned down—and I expect she chose someone with a sports car.

Ascending from Little Langdale, Wrynose seems reasonable to the local driver. The stranger may feel slightly squeamish about the drop on the left. To pack animals it should have been no hardship, although antiquarians hint at their suffering by claiming that the ancient spelling of 'Wrynose' was 'vreini hals', the pass of the stallion, where the animals tended to fall and break their teeth. 'Raven hause', the home of the raven, sounds more convincing. Had it to be named again, I would christen it with some title involving water, for in soaking weather the fells supporting the summit are laced by a ballet of new becks, twisting, twining, leaping, water in its most triumphant and abandoned ecstasies.

The reverse slope itself of Wrynose gives less anxieties to the timid. But the natural threats, in liquid weather, are more serious. The slopes of Greyfriar, dominating this side, have large gullies vulnerable to frost. The thaw loosens the stone. Torrential rain brings an occasional avalanche. In 1966 an enormous mass of scree and boulder tore down the fell-breast, removed a slice of the road as a spoon can remove the top of an egg, and finally came to chaotic rest on the far side, where the baby Duddon bubbles down to the valley. A walk among that clutter of rock was a sobering experience. I would like—from a safe place—to have seen the actual avalanche.

Where the foot of Wrynose and the foot of Hardknot meet stands the farmhouse of Cockley Beck. In the lasting snows of early 1947 the family here were marooned, in the sense that the farmer and his brother were just able to cut a passage through the snow wide enough to admit their bodies. At the start of the thaw in Eskdale I walked over Hardknot and looked down into the massy whiteness of Dunnerdale. At one point I came to a drift quite 20 feet deep, skirted it, and presently reached Cockley Beck. The farmer's wife opened the door, smiled widely, and talked like a mountain torrent. Next, she apologized, explaining that apart from the family I was the first person she had spoken to for six weeks.

The bridge divides Cockley Beck, in Lancashire, from Blackhall, in Cumberland, a farm set high above its lengthy lonnin. A previous owner, Ralph Tyson, became a legend in his life-time. I heard a lot about this giant from an Eskdale dalesman who knew him well, himself no dwarf. For a year Ralph lived where I live now, and so my Eskdale friend was able to give a practical demonstration of the giant's size. He pointed and said: 'See yon doorway.'

I nodded. Its height was six feet three. He said. 'T'old chap hed to bend head and turn sideways to git through. Aye.'

Great he was in bulk and years, for he lived from 1820 until 1918. Even when his sons were in their fifties they had to walk behind him, and generally pay deference. He did his shopping in Coniston, plodding over from Dunnerdale by the Walna Scar track, and at 90 he treated the journey as a stroll. The nicest true story about the man deals with the Eskdale and Ennerdale Hunt.

'Ah was about twelve,' said my Eskdale friend, 'and he was ninety-yan or two. Hunt met near our spot, and t'old chap was there. Hounds put oop a fresh fox. By—! did yon fox move! We fairly ratched aboot fells till nigh midday. 'Twas nay easy to keep oop wi' Tyson.'

He smiled reminiscently, wagged his head. 'A fair capper was t'old chap. Hounds lost scent fur a bit. We stood aboot, like. He asked me if ah was hungered. Then he pulls oot o' pocket a couple o' biscuits, an' tells me they're his own baking.'

'Well?'

He went on to explain that he accepted one from Tyson, took a bite, and thought it was made of granite. Awaiting his chance until the old man happened to be looking the other way, he furtively knapped the biscuit against a boulder with the hope of breaking off a fragment, but the attempt was a failure.

'Ah turned back, an' there was t'old chap chawin' his like a bit o' sponge cake.'

Gleaming below Blackhall, the river Duddon curves past a steep, rocky 'how', crudely fortified in the dark ages, and still conjuring up an effect of ancient, grim defence, softened by the young trees recently planted by the Forestry Commission. Forestry here has paid courteous deference to the lonely loveliness of Dunnerdale. The right trees are in the right places, and the properly barren crags left barren. The whiteness of becks tears down between dark rock and light leafage. Despite the planting, this upper part of the dale yet hints at bleakness until the Duddon gushes under that toy from Ruritania, Birks Bridge. The transformation is immediate, startling. Thence onwards even the steep and solitary suggest that they might just possibly approve the presence of human beings.

Between two and three miles downstream of Birks, sizeable stepping stones mark the Duddon. There used to be posts on either bank with a loose wire supposed to assist the passage across the river. It wavered and wobbled, and in days of semi-spate the timid dared not risk the crossing. After the collapse of the posts, somebody fixed the wire to two trees, by no means in line with the stepping stones. The place is called Fiddle or Fickle Steps, and both names are apt, for at high water, what with the wire swaying away from the frantic hand and the feet slipping off the wet stones, the venture is a blend of fiddling and gambling. On an occasion of this type, with a middle-aged couple and two girls in their late teens, I suggested that the safest way to cross would be by wading. So we took off our boots and socks, and paddled over knee deep. While we were drying our feet on the other side, voices reached us, and a young man and a very pretty girl in a jersey and navy slacks appeared on the opposite bank. She began to cross by the stones, with a kind of untroubled grace, swayed, tilted at an impossible angle as the wire sagged further away, and fell in.

The man with me said compassionately: 'Oh, hard luck!'

That, too, was my pitying sentiment.

The middle-aged woman said: 'Serve her right. She was showing off.' One of the teenagers said: 'Yes, showing off to her young man.'

The other said: 'Yes, and to us as well.'

Had it been the young man who fell in, would we two males have been so callous? Probably.

Little has changed along this dale since Wordsworth wandered here in his school holidays. I like to think of him staring at the challenge of Wallowbarrow Crag, or standing in the silence of Seathwaite Church and marvelling at the strength and simplicity of Wonderful Walker, the parson who in his own sphere fairly rivalled Ralph Tyson. These days folk wonder why the Church generally seems to be losing its hold. My own wonder is, would the Church keep its grip if all our clergy were like wonderful Walker? I believe the answer is Aye, but an almost impossible Aye. He helped with the sheep and the crops, spun his own wool, taught the children, doctored the sick, refused preferment, and on a stipend of ten pounds a year, plus tiny payments for serving as a part-time labourer, managed to save £2,000. Even today, I suppose, this kind of marvel might be wrought in a remote rural community. But the rest of England is beyond such miracles.

The Newfield Inn, which is old, and bakes scones that taste like being kissed by an angel, awaits you around the bend, west of the church. It can direct you to the memorial bridge over the Duddon and the track that scrambles up the flank of Wallowbarrow Crag. All about here crowds beauty—attended, in high summer, by the Beast. Ants, wood-ants, trillions of trillions of them, are working deedily, bringing up their eggs to get the benefit of the sun, taking them down to escape the cool shadow of the cloud, carting and shoving and tugging bits of stick, bits of leaf, sometimes along the flat, sometimes, and for no apparently intelligent reason, up one side of a huge boulder and down the other. Much as I abominate notices, I almost, but not quite, feel that the authorities should put up warning boards 'Take Heed Where you Sit.'

At Ulpha, five miles further downstream, the very name suggests, if not magic casements opening upon faerie seas forlorn, at least more engrossing miles to be visited, and by road there are three choices, the hill clambering up past the Traveller's Rest, or the two forks a short way beyond Ulpha Church. The left fork over the bridge enters Lancashire. The right, growing steep and narrow, heads for Corney Fell, for huge views, for sheep and more sheep, for farms that dwell beyond remoteness. There are ruins where, at the dark of night and in howling winds, even the very best fiends must feel a trifle on edge. There is a new bridge, the Logan Beck, built by the Cumberland roadmen, which does them great credit and truly belongs to the scene; by the side of it they left unharmed the old, double-section bridge that might have been designed for a delicately imaginative pantomime.

A little way further on a signpost makes the fortunate walker or driver say: 'How happy could I be with either.' To the left the road descends past Duddon Hall. To the right it swings up and up and yet up, and I suggest that the simplest answer to the problem of choice is to be greedy. Go down to Duddon Hall first, but leave enough daylight for the view over the fell.

Opposite Duddon Hall the wall flanking the road has been built as a low terrace, where you may sit and conjure up romance. The building crumbles, and the wildly dramatic pavilion in the park peels with decay. The chapel, for Divine Worship on Sundays and cock-fighting on weekdays, is damp and shadowy. The grounds themselves vainly demand a host of gardeners. And yet, with the great trees, and the distant, placid reach of the Duddon, and the fell beyond mounting towards smiling mystery, life and death seem to have effected a compromise, for nothing here frightens, nothing saddens.

Several ghosts are reputed to have residence at Duddon Hall, and that, surely, is not surprising.

Come back up to Corney Fell, idle a while, and watch the sheep. They are heaf-bred, that is to say, prepared by inherited instinct to keep reasonably within the limits of their own fell-grazing stints. As August sheep, their worries are few. Grazing is plentiful, and the lambs are growing big enough to look after themselves, though they still snatch an occasional suckle, more as a symbol than refreshment. Although not quite so vital to the Lake District as they were once, sheep are yet the life-blood of fell-farming. Millions of words must have been written about the lakes themselves. Sheep deserve as many. As for their history, I feel they may have been founder-members of the Creation. They were an ancient race when the Romans built their fort on Hardknot. Perhaps the legionaries received an issue of sheepskin jackets to keep out the wickedness of the winter. Sheepskin dating from that period was dug up there recently.

Stupid, cunning, timid, aggressive, spineless, enduring, enraging, amusing, all these adjectives and more apply to the ovine breed. They merit the interest of the visitor, and sometimes put on a performance worth gate-money. I do sincerely wish that townsfolk could have met Ada. She was a frowsty old yow, half-Herdwick, half-Swaledale, her fleece ragged and a poor colour. She mumbled

to herself, and browsed in a queerly, irritable manner.

On a morning early in May, in the field immediately east of our farmhouse, she lay sprawled close to the wall, her lamb at her side. The Hunt had met a mile further down the dale. The fox they put up, quick and clever, slid into some beck, shook off the scent, and came pattering up the road with no urgency. A young chap emerging from the byre spied it and let out the shrill, ululating cry that has but one meaning in these parts. Reynard leapt the wall, missing Ada by inches. With an enraged whicker she was on her hoofs and delivering a hearty butt. Startled, and well shaken, he made for the far gate, Ada after him. As he cleared the top bar she mumbled sourly, and went back to her lamb. By now hounds were lolloping up the road. Following scent, they jumped the wall in one's and two's where Reynard had jumped, Ada launching herself at them time and again. She deserved a public with rosettes and rattles.

The southern view from Corney Fell suggests a series of gigantic waves, growing higher and higher towards the far skyline. The walker can safely do as he pleases. The motorist suffers the dangerous temptation of craving to look back. Let him pull in and stare to his eyes' content. For full measure the south-east offers the Druid Circle of Swinside near the farm in the hollow, and further on the gold and platinum sheen of the Duddon estuary.

The summit of this generous road must be in close partnership with the weather, for it played a subtle trick on us. We were a party of three, two men and a woman who had lived in this tall quietude long ago and ached to see it once again. We had left the coast in amiable brilliance. Soon scarves of mist drifted over, wove together into a dank, dun pall. Visibility shortened to almost 30 yards, and the air grew chill. It was mournfully bad luck on our woman passenger. Not daring to hope, we edged on slowly. All we could see were nearby small boulders, bents and seeves poking damply through the margins of the mist. I knew the road well enough to judge that the summit loomed near.

There was not even a rustle of air. The mist simply dispersed in a flick under the Almighty Conjuror's hand. There they were, those rolling, rising fells, pallid lilac and primrose and dove grey under the sunlight. Sheep wandered and browsed, and slept, and a solitary crow perched and cawed on a fretted jumble of rocks. Behind us the Irish Sea was azure, polished and limitless.

CHAPTER SEVEN

September

My earliest recollection of Windermere is of a picture in a school geography book. It looked large, lovely and peaceful. It remains large, for ten and a half miles is a sizeable sheet of water, lovely, but not always peaceful. Traffic here and there has a congestion reminiscent of the south. Ambleside, Windermere, Bowness can well-nigh seethe with visitors in the busy season. The steamers that ply on the lake, and provide the best means of viewing it, are what Westmerians would call thrang with passengers. Yet anybody seeking solitude can find it easily either along lanes or on the fells. An enterprising car, dawdling around the perimeter, through Troutbeck Bridge and Bowness, past Cartmel Fell, Lakeside, Newby Bridge and back via Graythwaite and Far Sawrey ought to discover peaceful side issues. The walker on Claife Heights should have beauty to himself.

Windermere must have been the first of the lakes to be patronized by the late Georgians. It met their requirements of scenic charm without too much Gothic horror, water, fine trees, reasonably non-terrifying hills. Wealthy North Country folk, especially Mancunians, built large houses and laid out handsome gardens near the shores. The trend to criticize these in recent years strikes me as hollow impertinence. Most of our modern architecture would look monstrous in the Lake District, crude geometry and concrete hugging each other in tasteless embrace. A touring New Zealander, sharing with me admiration of a fine old house, said:

'That's great. That's lovely. That's what we come to see. So do

Australians and Americans. Why don't your authorities realize it? Why don't they preserve the old stuff, instead of knocking it down and sticking up square ugliness? Doesn't your tourist trade count for anything?'

He had been cruising around Windermere, enjoyed crossing on the ferry, glanced appreciatively at Belle Isle and the lesser islands, and smiled at the general views. Although his own land was green, he reckoned this to be greener. What gladdened him most were ancient farmhouses and cottages. He pointed out that back home they had nothing much older than 1860. To us the date is so recent that, sometimes waking up blearily, I feel I was born in that year.

I suggested that he should inspect the Washington window, once in Cartmel Priory, North Lancashire, and now in the parish Church of St. Martin, at Bowness. Dating from 1403, it commemorates George Washington's 12th ancestor, John, and the arms include the Stars and Stripes. The New Zealander was intrigued to learn of the close connection between the Lake District and the U.S.A. and wanted to know the cause of it. My own theory is that Whitehaven provided the rational bond. As the third port in England, until Liverpool grew up, its natural market was America. Prosperous Cumbrian business men went to and fro in the small sailing ships, and some of the captains, incidentally, brought back the *araucaria* or monkey puzzle, now big trees and weirdly out of place on some of the fell-farms.

George Washington's grandmother was a Whitehaven woman. Some of his male ancestors went to school at Penrith. Bringing the link to a much later date, President Woodrow Wilson's mother was the daughter of a Carlisle clergyman. The memorial plaque on the church in Lowther Street is worth a glance.

There is a great deal to be said for Windermere as a holiday resort. Apart from the scenery there are such shrines as Beatrix Potter's house at Sawrey. To me the average museum, however interesting, is dead. Her small house lives, intimately, in a way that appeals to all nice children, young or grown-up.

Mentioning children, if they are restive from excessive scenery and confinement in the back of the car, take them to the sea one fine day. It belongs to Lakeland as much as the fells.

There may be some official geographer who can define exactly the boundaries of the Lake District, but I have yet to find him. On the west the Solway shore has as much right to inclusion as the inland waters, for the rivers and becks emerging from these fan out into lonely, lovely estuaries. Some stretches, such as the coastline running past Whitehaven and Workington, despoiled by ancient and ruined industries, might have been the inspiration of that hymn line 'where only man is vile'. Others remain almost unknown, quiet symphonies of sea-washed Cumberland turf and damp platinum sand, far from any road. Did I say quiet? Here the red-beaked, red-legged oyster catcher pipes with the insistence of Ravel's *Bolero*. Gulls and terns and waders swoop and strut and paddle on their lawful occasions. A small, infrequent train keeps close to the sea, and has this world of birds to itself. It must be the most befeathered section of line in the kingdom.

One glinting September afternoon I was going down to a farm near Seascale to inspect a second-hand muck-spreader.

Eb said: 'Ah's nay been yonder fur a gey lang while.'

'Right. Hop in.'

An hour or so later, the air warm and washed, we were tasting our leisure on the beach, the Isle of Man sprawled as a grey-blue invitation along the rim of the sea, and the Galloway shores to the north conjuring up thoughts of some secret venture. A few miles behind us reared up the panoply of the western fells, Gable and the Scafells, the stark, swart Screes pitching down into Wastwater.

The tide was out, and Eb jerked a horny thumb seawards.

'A chap maun (must) git tired walkin' oot there afore he wets his feet.'

I laughed and reminded him that at some of these places the turn of the tide could teach an arrogant man a lesson. At Ravenglass, for instance, the ford near the shore seems a mere dribble at low water. Wait a short while after the turn of the tide, and the dribble swells to a menacing surge.

'Ever been to Arnside, Eb?'

'Aye, yance (once).'

We agreed that the tide at Arnside was a terror. Loll on the beach a minute or two before the end of the ebb and blink sleepily across wide sands marked by a shallow, gentle channel. Fall asleep for five minutes, and God help you. The water surges in, frothing and hissing, the cables of anchored boats threaten to snap, and a human body in that flood becomes a straw.

Eb nodded soberly. 'Aye, enough to mek (make) an otter fleyt (frightened).'

We idled along the narrow verge of greenery on the seaward side of the railway line. Because of the bank, the chimneyed clutter of atomic Sellafield, a mile or so north, remained invisible. This slim privacy of herbage flanking the beach quivered and shimmered with wild flowers, for no man bothered about it, and it had escaped the curse of chemical spraying. A south-west breeze fluttered gently, stirring a great oasis of dog-roses flourishing in the sand itself. Over the tiniest flowers beneath the bank hovered five-spot burnets. The warmth, the quietude, the distant stillness of the Solway, the silver and scarlet of the burnets produced a sensation I can describe only in hackneyed words as of time standing still.

Eb stared at those darkish silver wings with their scarlet spots. 'Gey bonnie, them.'

'You've seen them before, surely?'

'Nay.'

I was back in Devon, a boy of nine, watching the burnets on a drowsy August day in Budleigh Salterton. I was remembering a grown-up friend showing me how easily they could be coaxed with the fingertips. Could I do it again?

In a tentative fashion I began to explain to Eb, and he gave me a doubting glance.

'There now,' he said, like a mother humouring an over-imaginative child.

It was a challenge. 'Anyway,' I told him, 'I'll have a go.'

Very slowly and softly the middle fingertips of my right hand stroked the base of a slender stem. The burnet on the petals above took no notice. Eb raised surprised brows. I forgot the distant fells climbing skywards to the east of me, and the lilac Solway shimmering sleepily to the west, forgot everything but my fingertips, the cool, green stem and a ridiculously delicate and gay little creature resting on a petal. Nearer, nearer, stroking, nearer. The crisis was here. The pads of my fingertips stroked upwards another fraction of an inch, and then I was holding aloft my hand, moving it up and down and around, bearing a fashion parade of an untroubled, brilliant little burnet.

'Look at those spots,' I whispered.

'Gocks! 'Tis a fair marvel how them laal beauties git made.'

The burnet offered no attempt to fly off. I felt flattered, humbly proud, yet almost superhuman. I was reminded of that delicious book *The Maker of Heavenly Trousers* in which a fastidious young Khan of Turkestan persuades butterflies to rest on his fingernails.

With more stealthy gentleness I lowered my hand to a blossom, stroked my fingers over its silkiness, and left the burnet to its own flimsy enchantment.

Eb smiled, slowly and widely. 'Aye,' he said, 'aye. 'Tis summat gey different fra handlin' a mook-spreader.'

Whereas spoken dialect, even though utter gibberish, is usually amusing to the listener, printed dialect can be irksome. To omit it entirely from a book of this nature would be foolish. Lakeland talk, varying a lot within its own confines, has the dignity of an almost separate language. It is not simply a matter of pronunciation but of a different vocabulary. The older folk, talking among themselves, use a large percentage of Norse. Many of the place-names have Norse terminations—keld (spring), thwaite (clearing), garth (rough field), holme (stead), wath (ford). The very word fell is Norwegian, the economical Cumbrian leaving out the 'j' from *fjell*.

Until recently a local man with a good ear could listen to a Lakelander and identify his dale, or village, or town. Even these days of radio-ridden and televized uniformity, the ordinary greeting differs between a dale and the coast a few miles off. In the dale, one says to another: 'Hoo's fettle? (How's your condition? i.e. how are you?)' On the coast it would be: 'Hoo's marrer? (How's your mate?)'— a curious legacy from the close companionship of miners.

My first visit to Whitehaven landed me in lingual bewilderment.

Searching for the Gents, I asked an elderly man. Baffled by his answer, I pretended to be rather deaf, and asked if he would mind repeating his directions. Baffled a second time, I had no option but to say: 'I'm awfully sorry, but I just can't understand.' He chuckled, took me by the arm, and led me there. That same callow year I was out with Will Porter in a car, driving to Watendlath to collect some foxhound puppies. Will enjoyed chatting, but naturally paused on occasion, waiting for a comment on his remarks. Not having the remotest idea of what he had been saying, I invented a word sounding like 'M'yerh', easily interpreted as either Yes or No. Next day I started to learn the language.

There were the technical words, such as the sheep vocabulary, yow for ewe, tup or tip for ram, gimmer for female, hogg for growing lamb, shearling for once-clipped sheep, twinter for sheep two winters old, wether for doctored ram. There were the musical, compact expressions such as harksta (listen), looksta (look you). There were the variations on the word 'you'. 'Thou' and 'thee' explain themselves. 'Thu' was more subtle. It struck me as usually employed when the speaker wanted to convey annoyance. Belonging to this archaic yet satisfying branch of the dialect are the grand old verbs that have dropped out from our emasculated B.B.C. English. A dog will rive away at a bone, and on the job of gathering sheep he will get the order 'Bide!'

'Aye' and 'nay' somehow have more depth and sincerity than 'Yes' and 'No'. The Northern version may give amusement to the keeping-up-with-the-Jones visitor, refained enough to talk about 'breown ceows'. A short story of mine, set in the Lake District, was submitted to a woman's magazine published in London. The fastidious editress liked the story, and added: 'There's just one thing, D'you mind if I change a few words in the dialogue? I'm sure no nice girl would say "Aye".' I retaliated by asking her if she had ever heard those nasty Common(s) M.P.'s using the same term.

With us, 'Where is he?' becomes 'Wheer's he at?' Nobody says 'I think so' but 'Aye, likely.' 'Gey' or very, is one of the props of North Country chatter. Without it, most of us dalesfolk would be lost. Another use of the word gave sudden happiness to a pretty

young Cumberland girl. She had come as a waitress to a hotel where I was staying in Westmorland. Though her home was a mere few miles away, over the county border, she felt terribly homesick. Then she met a Westmorland lad. A few days later, bringing my morning tea, her eyes were shining.

'He's sicca (such a) chap,' she said softly. 'Last night he said to me. 'Ista geyly?' I'd nivver heard that before.'

He was asking her, in two words, was she feeling as sweet as she looked.

Words beginning with a vowel are often prefixed with a 'y'. Oak becomes 'yak' and acre 'yakker'. The word 'yat' for 'gate' recalls Symons Yat above the Severn. Perhaps this is a far-off legacy from the tongue of the Ancient British, refugees to Cumbria, Wales, Cornwall and Brittany. 'Yan' meaning 'one', 'once' is inevitably pronounced 'yance'. A little boy I know, son of one of the few Lakeland farmers to move south, on his first day at the new school had really bad luck. The subject was English, and the book to be read aloud was a fairy story. The little boy's surname began with A, and so he found himself having to open the proceedings. Slowly and deedily he read out: 'Yance upon a time—'

To the uninitiated an excess of dialect can become boring. I beg forgiveness for using up a few more lines on the subject. After all, September is a month of Shows, and to attend one or two, and listen, and pick out the meaning here and there of a 'crack' being enjoyed by a bunch of farmers and shepherds, that is something of a triumph. Would you care to learn to count up to 20? Yan, tan, tethera, methera, pimp, sethera, lethera, hovera, dovera, dick, yan-a-dick, tan-a-dick, tethera-dick, methera-dick, bumfit, yan-a-bumfit, tan-a-bumfit, tethera-bumfit, methera-bumfit, gigot.

Or you might prefer a few phrases like:

'Ista gaan til baith them meadas? (Are you going to both those fields?).'

'A bit uv a stir (a party).'

'He's oop rake behint intek. (He's up the fell track behind the enclosure.)'

Armed with these modest fragments of dialect, attend one of the

Shows, Sheep Show, Puppy Show, any kind of show connected with a dale. September is a popular month for them, and if Windermere has nothing available while you are there, find one elsewhere by consulting a local paper.

The first item worth study when you enter the ground is the feet of the men. Some will be wearing clogs, some shepherds' boots. There is much merit in both. Except in very hot weather, when the wooden insulation is a drawback, I wore clogs for years, the uppers of leather shaped like a boat, the wooden soles protected by caulkers, rims of steel fixed around the edges. My first pair cost twenty-three and sixpence. They kicked rocks and hurt the rocks. They kept my feet bone dry while I worked for a week in a beck that had become dangerous to sheep, standing in the slush and carving out seeves and bog-myrtle and sodden moss. In snowy weather I tacked pieces of rubber from an inner tube on to the soles, otherwise the snow would have stuck to them in coagulated lumps. The second pair, much more extravagant, were thirty-five shillings and modestly elegant—though not so showy as the Sunday clogs still worn by some of the bairns, gay footwear studded with ornamental brass and threaded with coloured laces.

Shepherds' boots are aristocrats, of fine quality leather, laced down almost to the tip of the toe, to prevent cracking and to give an extra springy effect. The toes are turned up at such an angle, the wearer ascending the fell simply takes a pace forward and the boot steps up almost under its own volition. The style is known as duck neb (beak) with plenty of tummel (curve). Ironmongery on sole and heel vary according to the taste of the wearer. A large friend of mine, his fell-grazing stint spread across the most boulder-strewn, scree-ridden tilts in the Lake District, had a pair that weighed eleven pounds. They are expensive, and worth it. Give a shepherd good boots, a good crook, and a good dog, and happiness is there.

Go over to the sheep pens and pretend to discriminate between the standard of the entries. Those massive animals raddled pink, with thick, boldly curving horns and white, lion-like faces are Herdwick tups. Their horns are oiled, and their faces have likely received a dab of powder. The little dales' boys inspecting them probably know as much about the subject as implied by their deedy manner. That huge tethered bull, sprawled on the ground, the rosette of the first prize attached to its headstall, is so fat, you can venture to pat it.

Across in the Women's Institute tent there is a hum of talk, a scent of flowers mixed with that of damp canvas, and an enticing hint of newly baked cakes and bread. Resist the temptation to sneak a piece of bacon and egg pie. Quieten your lust by judging the children's painting and handwriting competitions, or the entries for the floral decoration section. Before you emerge and glance across the field to the serrated vista of the distant fells, a washed undulation of gold and lilac and shadowed indigo, remember to admire the display of professionally made crooks, inviting pieces of local timber and carved sheephorns.

That high yell is a reminder that the hound-trail for dogs will be starting in a few minutes. Watch the beginning, then hurry over to the spot where young fellows are gathering in vests and shorts. Some wear boots and some—those with reliable ankles—shoes. In front of them, beyond a stone wall and a knobbly spread of rough ground daubed with whins, the fell rises steeply, a scratchy little track curving up between boulders, sparse bents, brackens. Next, the track enters a gully, narrow, extra steep, the bed of it coated with soft, squelching moss, the devil's own impediment to any living creature in a hurry. Beyond that again obtrude shelves of crags, and above them the ground quietens to a steep bank stippled by bents. Up there, a thousand feet above the contestants, squats a man by a flag.

There are eleven entries, all of them dales-born. Guide- or fell-racing belongs to those who have tackled the steeps almost daily since they were toddlers. Some of them have a shepherd's heart, with a slow beat. The eleven line up in a casual manner, the handkerchief drops, and they sprint for the wall. On the other side they run across the rough ground. Approaching the base of the gully, a broad-shouldered lad in a blue shirt is leading. Once inside the tormenting gradient of the gully, he drops to a brisk walk, hands on knees, while spectators from the plains watch and gasp for breath.

The confines of the gully are such, Blueshirt is bound to lead for a while.

He emerges, scrambles among the crags, followed closely by a lad in red shorts. Of the eleven, nine are close and the other two lagging. Blueshirt trots around the flag, and a visitor glances at his watch, lets out a sort of incredulous sigh, and says: 'Seven and a half minutes! I'd have been proud to do it in half an hour.'

Blueshirt is running down, and now jumping from crag to crag, feet together to avoid the risk of rupture. Redshorts is nearing him. Whoever reaches the gully first seems certain to be the winner. Blueshirt gets there, runs, slides, stumbles, tears down the course of the gully. Behind him, Redshorts loses his foothold. Slap on his backside he goes, slithers and toboggans through wet moss and over knobbly scree, gains half a second by the accident, pelts after Blueshirt while the watchers yell and bellow their support. They are dead level coming over the rough ground, and the wall will be the decider. Redshorts leaps, grabs, makes a swinging vault over the top, and races home with two yards to spare. There his pal passes him his jacket, and he takes out a cigarette and lights it while the visitors from the plains are still panting with wonder.

Wrestling comes on about five o'clock. There is one all-important rule. If any part of a contestant, except his feet, touches the ground, then he is the loser. The rule makes for fair play, good humour, and a swift, scientific adjustment of balance that would do credit to a ballet dancer. Not that strength is unimportant. During the last century exponents of Cumberland and Westmorland wrestling cultivated immense muscles. In a book entitled *Wrestliana* there are photos of the ancient champions, and like the Army Physical Training Staff of the old days, these men are so overdeveloped, their arms are unable to fall straight. By the Edwardian period Swedish methods were coming into their own, and speed and agility counted as much as muscle.

The young boys are first in the ring, some of the lads so little they find it hard to obtain the compulsory grip of one arm over and one under the opponent's shoulder, the fingers of each hand gripping together. A flick, a twist, and one is on the ground. He jumps up and leans forward for the next hod. His opponent, long-armed and quiet, tightens and heaves, and that is that.

Although most of these 'hods' are over quickly, an occasional exception stills the watchers in a long-drawn spell of excitement. During an All-Weights bout one competitor, like a giant blacksmith, looked capable of crushing his opponent to pulp. But the giant was a little slow, and the other man quick as an eel. With a squeezing shove of his great arms the giant swept his man off the ground. Intending to swing him down, he was a tenth of a second too late. A curving foot shot out, clamped hard behind the giant's knee. There they were in deadlock, each waiting for the other to make a move. The giant's balance, threatened by knee-pressure, was hair-trigger. For minutes, it seemed, the two remained in tableau, paralysed, and then the giant made a terrific heave, swung his man, lost his balance. As the two fell, the lighter man twisted himself on top. Goliath, genial Goliath, lay there and grinned his admiration.

Grinning reminds me that there may be a 'gurning' competition, still popular at some of the Shows. The competitor sticks his face through a horse collar, and with the illumination of candles held on either side, makes a nightmare grimace. Judging is based on the volume of laughter from the audience. Egremont Crab Fair specializes in this jovial absurdity, and also in another that demands heroic qualities. This is the unholy business of smoking a new pipe filled with strong tobacco. Singing and shouting competitions have rather fallen behind in the last few years. The shouting is based on the idea of a shepherd or farmer calling his distant dog. I once heard Will Porter calling his pack in a valley separated from mine by a ridge a thousand feet high, and in the last shouting competition to which I listened the winner was a farmer's wife whose call reached an official a mile away.

Not all Shows stage Sheepdog Trials, possibly because the standards are expected to be high, and many a working dog, calmly competent and intelligent on its own fell, appears to get confused by the presence of an audience. The 'professional' Trial dogs, as they might be termed, enjoy applause, and will make a circuit of the course at the bidding of their trainer, plainly enjoying themselves.

What they might achieve on a rough and ready fell is a matter of guessing. A neighbour of mine, whose fell stint includes a wall of dizzy crags crossed by the narrowest of trods, has dogs that behave with human wisdom. Once the driven sheep are close to the trod, the dogs freeze, giving the sheep an untroubled passage across the dangerous trod. When the yows are over, the dogs lope across and take charge.

As I see it, a steady pace without fuss or bother is vital to a Trials dog. Down it trots, collects its three sheep, steers them round here, round there, and presently is guiding them towards the pen where the owner stands, holding the rope on the gate with one hand and an out-stretched stick in the other. If the pace is quiet and unchanging the sheep seem to slip inside as if they belonged there. But there are sheep and sheep. The most uproarious Trials episode I ever witnessed happened years ago not far from Workington. I have told the story before, and make no apology for repeating it. Three wild and woolly sheep were released, and the owner ordered his dog down to gather them. Two were subservient, but the third strolled off in disdain. Angrily the owner sent the dog back to gather it. This time the sheep stood still with a remarkable effect of bored contempt. The dog, a 'fixer', crouched belly to earth and started a hypnotic crawl towards its quarry. When the dog was about five yards short, the sheep launched a butt, sent the dog sprawling. The infuriated owner shouted and whistled. The dog took a final look, seemed to shake its head, and walked the other way. The defiant sheep made for the entrance. Two officials stood there, knee to knee, shooing and waving it back in lordly fashion. The crowd waited eagerly, praying for the worst, and their prayer was granted. The sheep charged, caught each official on one knee, knocked them both flat, and careered into the field beyond. Such ovine thuggery warms the heart.

Sheep Shows, Puppy Shows and the like have a natural affinity with food. Apart from the fact that Man Must Eat, there are the W.I. cookery competitions, the savoury entries so perfect, so appetizing, the theft of an apple cake or a bacon and egg pie would be deemed by a wise magistrate pardonable provocation. Lake District eating has never been on the sparse side, even in the days of rationing.

Officialdom did its utmost to turn cream and butter and ham into nostalgic visions of yesteryear, but farmers had their ways of defeating the law. After the Spartan diet of southern towns, Cumbrian hospitality was both manna and tantalizing, because some of us lost the ability to be anything but Spartan. Capacity had shrivelled.

Soon after the War I went with a Cumberland friend to visit a Windermere farmer on business. Not wanting to cadge a meal in those tight-waisted days, we took sandwiches with us. But the farmer's wife insisted that we should stay to Sunday dinner. A large jug of burnet wine was on the table, made from a flower that produces a drink resembling port. Confronted by a plate of roast beef sufficient for three, I dared not hurt her feelings by leaving anything. The next course consisted of two dishes, one a trifle topped by four inches of whipped cream, and the other a beasting's pudding made from the milk of a newly calved cow. I tried to refuse both. She refused my refusal, and spooned out a great helping of trifle. I managed it somehow, and found myself subsiding into a sated coma.

Out to the kitchen she went again, and returned with a huge tray. On one side was the tea. On the other were various dishes, apple cake, scones spread thickly with rum butter, and that sweet confection known locally as 'sudden de-ath (death)', a double layer of pastry lined with currents enriched with date juice. I groaned, and shook my head. She looked at me with pity and said: 'There maun be summat wrong. Thou's nay appetite at all.'

Since the stomach is claimed to be the seat of emotions, and the stomach and food are close friends, perhaps this is the place to mention traditions and superstitions. Although the funeral of a dalesman is not quite so controlled by custom as it used to be, there is still a measure of ancient ritual. Wait with me by the gate, among a quiet crowd of local folk. The men are dark-clad, some wearing ancient bowler hats. As the cortège approaches, escorted by the mourning family and relations, we draw back a little. In the lapels of some are sprigs of boxwood. The bell tolls, and between the mournful notes is the sound of the nearby river murmuring, and the incurious whicker of a yow in the adjoining field. In slow procession we follow the coffin up the path to the porch. A tall, elderly man, close to the front, had the task of 'bidding' the mourners to be present.

After the interment we line up, and moving slowly, take our turn to look down into the grave. On the sunlit skirt of the fell beyond the river a meadow pipit is trilling. Presently we are back in the church lonnin, talking in modulated voices, and making our way by foot or car to the local, where there will be a ham tea. There may be fancy cakes as well, though these, until recently, were regarded as too frivolous for the occasion. No longer will there be arvel bread, formerly a kind of memorial food, to be taken home and given to those unable to attend the funeral.

The deceased kept bees, and this morning his elder brother went out to the hives, with wine and sweet butter and told them of the death. A decent, kindly chap, this elder brother, and firm in certain old beliefs. When the sick man lay a-dying in the farmhouse bedroom, close to his end, the parson called, and the elder brother barred his entry. There was no hostility about the act. It was simply that a parson, having a care of souls, might take this one away before it was finally ready to leave the body. It was the elder brother who had arranged the sin-eating rite, almost secretly, for fear of distressing the parson. Being unrelated, I was not bidden to this. The nearest and dearest gathered at one end of the kitchen. The dead man was placed on the kitchen table, a plate of bread and meat nearby. The sin-eater, an old man who is paid a modest fee, came in silently and ate the meal, so consuming the sins of the dead. God forbid that I should condemn this custom. Utter reverence was there, its significance close to that of Holy Communion. Surely no observance is wrong if the intent be clean and unselfish?

Who shall blame the Cumbrian girl who bowed twice during the Creed? Questioned about it, she said: 'T'second bow was fur Satan.'

'What!'

'Oo, aye. Ma moother tellt me oalas (always) to mek friends on baith (both) sides.'

Lighter traditions include the April noddie (fool) and the May gosling. In all probability the frightening increase in quantity and speed of transport has killed a custom once common in the smaller

villages and hamlets. If a young chap came courting from another parish, it was reckoned to be a form of poaching, and he had to pay his footing, both before he was wed and after.

The tragic outbreak of Foot-and-Mouth disease in the back-end of 1967, when the Lake District waited in dread lest the scourge should get on to the open fell and necessitate the slaughter of all those flocks, a disaster that the fell-farmers escaped by the skin of their teeth, recalls a remedy for dealing with this plague. It was called the Need-Fire, a usage forbidden by a canon of the Church, and mentioned in *Chronicon de Lanercost* about 1268. The farmer whose herd was infected or threatened would make a great fire of whins and brackens, damp enough to create thick smoke, and through this choking swirl he drove his beasts, in the belief that it purged the infection in the air. There is record of a Troutbeck farmer who went one stage further. To make assurance double sure, he also sent his wife through the Need-Fire.

CHAPTER EIGHT

October

Old-fashioned writers, describing an honest and friendly man, were fond of the expression 'an open countenance'. It applies to Bassenthwaite, the only sheet of water with the sub-title of Lake. Unshadowed by any imminent crags, it looks bright even on a dull day. In sunshine, sprinkled by the gay wings of small sailing-boats, it belongs more to the South than the stern North. Holiday traffic keeps busy the road on its eastern shore. The far bank stays quiet and sleepily charmed. Anybody who drives fast on this side should be condemned for life to a limit of 20 miles per hour. The very names alone condemn the absurdity of hurrying. Taking this route from the Portinscale end, you pass Dansing Beck in Applethwaite—which sounds like a line from a lyric. The late Graham Sutton lived here, a Cumbrian whose novels were soaked in the essence of the county.

Keswick itself has become a hive of visitors almost all the year round. It was known when most of the Lake District remained unknown. The literary and the fashionable favoured it with their presence. Its position is superb. But I call it a thousand pities that there was no great landowner to rebuild the town a hundred years ago, leaving gaps to gladden the eye with lordly views. I have no quarrel with the old buildings; not even with the new car park. It is simply that a place surrounded by such beauty ought to be able to see it at a glance. Such is the good fortune of Crosthwaite, on its fringe, where the old church reigns protectively over relics of history.

I would like to slip back through Time for a space and stroll about the town. It would be worthwhile just for the variety of the clothes, the elegance of the fashionable, the simplicities of the rural. Is that Southey making his way towards Greta Hall? He looks a little worried, and no wonder. His writing friends choose to sponge on him, and he is too kindly to kick them out. Is there any shadow across his mind, any dim dread of things to come? But how could he dream that one depressing day his wife will hang herself, a Cumbrian method of immolation as traditional as hara kiri in Japan.

That looks like Coleridge. Yes, it must be, perhaps recovering from a session of opium. Is his a case of addiction, or half-pretence? Odd to think that a century and more hence there will be a craze for dope among the younger generation.

Now, moving nearer to the present, I can see Hugh Walpole in his garden on the other side of Derwentwater. A successful and admired novelist, so successful that a farmhouse bears the announcement 'Judith Paris lived here', an achievement comparable in fame with the immortal Sherlock's Baker Street address. And yet I feel that the Lake District never got into Walpole's blood stream.

From the author to the pencil is a very tiny leap. The old pencil factory on the Greta deserves a smiling bow. This was the birth-place of the true lead pencil, known to the world as the *crayon d'anglais*. It came about because of the discovery of wad, black lead, up the narrowness of Borrowdale. To the owners of the precious stuff it meant a fortune, almost equivalent to the wealth of a diamond-mine, and involving similar problems of security. There had to be permanent armed guards, and armed escorts for wad in convoy. One arch-bandit bought ground nearby, and employed men to dig underneath until they broke through to his neighbour's wad. An exciting, filibustering phase it was, attended by small battles, and smuggling along secret trods across the fells. For a while the pencil makers flourished, and well they deserved to, producing pencils of such quality, the most doggedly illiterate might crave to write with them. Imagine the feel of cedar-wood between your fingers, and the wad making its flowing way across thick white paper.

Cheap foreign graphite began to intrude, affecting the trade, but the Keswick pencil still holds an honourable place, and the new factory further down the river is an efficient successor to the old.

October

Compared with West Lakeland, Keswick is sophisticated. In the nature of things, it had to be, and wisely following the policy of bigger towns, developed parks. One is mainly of turf and flanking trees, a glorified sports ground. The other has flowers and paths, and a bridge over the bubbling river, and like Friars Crag, may strike the dour, uncompromising fell-walker as too civilized for his exploring boots. So be it. Fitz Park and Friars Crag give sunshine and rest to large numbers who have another way of enjoying themselves.

In the summer Keswick holds its Convention. The Babel of many religions is to be heard, and tracts and pamphlets invite the passer to pause and consider, and no doubt it all helps this wicked world. A sardonic friend of mine told me a story I disbelieved about a brother of his, an idler who had failed at everything. Eventually he invented a new religion, launched it at Keswick, and retired on the proceeds. Though no doubt apocryphal, the idea could have stemmed from the quaint realities of the U.S.A. An American cousin of mine showed me a certificate, guaranteeing him a place in the Hereafter, which he had bought from a Hot Gospel society for five dollars.

The little Museum at Keswick, facing Fitz Park, is a gem. If you have only five minutes to spare, spend them here. Marvel at the astonishing piano made of beck-stones and wire, on the right, just beyond the entrance. Heaven knows how long it took to chip these slabs of stone until they attained the attuned precision of piano keys. A notice announcing PLEASE DO NOT TOUCH could hardly hope to cure the frailty of human nature. I used to pop in about two o'clock, the emptiest period, hide around a corner, and wait in anticipation. Sure enough some law-abiding citizen would enter, gaze at the piano, at the notice, glance furtively about to make sure he was alone, bang half a dozen notes out of the stone keys, and then hurry on. Now, I believe, visitors with honourable intentions are invited to have a go, and pleasant, stony tinkling is frequent.

There are old handbills of theatrical performances that gave huge value for very little money. A geological section, to the untutored, suggests that the bowels of the Lake District must be like Aladdin's cave. For stuffed birds and animals, so very dead and inevitably a little faded, I can never raise anything but a sense of depression. The literary manuscripts, fascinating because of their context, have an aspect that sometimes makes me ashamed, and sometimes slightly suspicious. They look so neat, so clean, so self-conscious. Have eminent writers an instinctive, almost sanitary tidiness? or maybe they say to themselves: 'H'm. This original MS ought to fetch a packet later on. I must be careful.'

Dear Old Keswick! in the high season a walker almost needs to turn sideways to edge through the crowds. About every fourth shop seems to be a café, or else selling gifts. Traffic crawls, the car parks are full, and I get a sudden urge to rush into the nearest isolation. From the main street this would be the pleasant grounds of Keswick School, where Southey's house stands on a tree-escorted bank. I could camouflage the trespass by pretending to be a parent.

Aye, dear old Keswick! I mean it. You are noisy, and commercial, and in winter your narrower streets are funnels of freezing shadow. But I like you. For better or for worse, you have always been synonymous with the Lake District. Besides, you are no more than an overgrown village, the hills at your doorstep, inexpressibly fine country mere minutes away. The American hustle-tourists who spend one night with you at least have a glimpse of your fells and your valleys. Whether they are at all clear about your geography is a different matter. I was staying in the town, and at breakfast shared a table with a most likeable, middle-aged American woman. She said:

'It's real pretty. But, say, where is this place called Cumberland?'

But for its popularity, Borrowdale would be the most beguiling of all. It twists and it turns, hints that around the next corner is the end, only to play a similar welcome trick again and again. These charms are unequalled elsewhere. Walk through it during a wet January day, and you may get delight almost to yourself. Most of the year cars and hikers inevitably make it less holy.

At Barrow House, a few miles out of Keswick, lived the late Bob Graham, first, so far as I know, of the big record breakers. He was powerfully built, modest, kindly, and as a sort of snack, after supper in the summer, he would skip up Skiddaw and back. In the early 1930's, during a fine spell, he left the market place at midnight on the Saturday, and arrived back just after 11.30 on the

Sunday night. He had covered the principal peaks, his foot mileage being 110 miles, and his total altitude 30,000 feet. He wore a vest, shorts, and canvas shoes with rope soles. Pacemakers, one per eight hours, accompanied him and fed him with greengages.

I asked him what really kept him going during the last eight hours.

He grinned and said: 'Will-power.'

Barrow House has falls, but better known are those of Lodore. In drenching weather they deserve the poem that was written about them. In drought a man might sit on them without being aware of it. To me, the name of Lodore is linked with something quite different from tumbling water. My first visit to the hamlet of Watendlath, reached from the valley by a fell road, was with a Cumberland farmer, a man of few words and given to understatement. He had some business with a sheep-farmer, and as we drove up and up, John jerked his thumb at the track leading away to the right.

'There's a gey bonnie view yon. On our way back we'll stop an' hev a leuk.'

Business completed, we drove back, stopped the car, and walked across to the view-point. When walking, John always carried a stick, and had the atrocious habit of resting the ferule on the very edge, folding his arms over the handle, and looking down. By the mercy of Fate and because we were using a car, he had no stick on this occasion. The sheer edge we reached made me step back a pace. He stood with the toes of his boots well over nothingness, staring into the depths.

Three well-built young women came walking up the rough road. They had never been this way before. One of them recognized him. Not dreaming that the branch track ended in space, she strode across, and before I could do anything, cried out: 'Hullo!' and slapped him heavily in the middle of the back.

Those old enough to recall Harold Lloyd wobbling on the window-ledges of skyscrapers may picture the scene. John swayed to and fro, and the moment seemed like a dozen seconds. At the same time the girl realized the truth, turned green, and fell backwards. Such was the shock, she started to cry.

'Oh, I—I—' Sobs were stifling her words. 'Oh, it's terrible! it's—'

'Aye,' he said, 'it's middlin'.'

Go through Rosthwaite, where one wicked night a great flood was poised to destroy the Skiddaw Hotel, and changed its course at the ultimate second. Rex, a dog that used to live here, took guests for walks. They had to keep exactly to the route he chose, or he barked until they obeyed him. Also, he prohibited folk from sitting down when they should have been on their feet. A friend of mine in Rex's charge, not caring to descend steepish slopes except on his behind, sat down to tackle an awkward pitch. Rex put his muzzle to my friend's ear and barked until he was forced to stand erect.

Past the turning to Honister the dale assumes a wildness. The last farm, Seathwaite, which holds the record rainfall for any inhabited place in England, points the way up to the Sty. Many an assault of water has it suffered, and in 1967 it was touch and go. The flood destroyed field walls and turned the stackyard into a beck. Once a friend and I deliberately walked there from Eskdale through rain storms, having arranged to be picked up by car and driven home via Keswick. As we were having tea in the kitchen, we were warned to get out in minutes, or the rising waters would trap the car. Back home, and stripping off my wet clothes, I found that some cheap blue braces had stained my back and front. The marks remained for a week. An Ancient Briton would have deplored my poor technique.

Return past the Honister road, cross the bridge at Grange and drive back to Keswick by the road on the other side of Derwentwater. This way is well-perched, airy, and provides a sensation of being superior. Presently, you may care to join the Newlands Pass. Should you long for more of Derwentwater, go on to Keswick, and the landing stages, and take a trip in one of the launches. Perhaps you will give a thought to that harmless and decent young man, the Earl of Derwentwater, beheaded for his part in the 1715 Rising, and to Charles, his brother, sentenced in his absence, and caught in a French ship and brought back and beheaded after the '45. They had reddish hair, and fine complexions, as the painting reveals in the Keswick Museum.

All around here is either sheep country or forestry. Interested visitors from the south ask endless questions about the sheep. Do they ever fall from a crag and get killed? Do they ever get stuck on a ledge? Do they ever lose themselves? Do they ever get stolen?

A sheep killed by the accident of falling is a rare event. A cragfast sheep is a different matter. Every year a few get trapped, for a foraging yow, spotting a few juicy blades on a ledge below, will leap down and then find herself marooned, because she cannot jump up as high as she can jump down. Blaring mournfully, she attracts attention.

As a lad, Eb was working in Borrowdale. A yow became cragfast, and two farmers and Eb started off to the rescue, carrying a couple of ropes and a sack. They reached the top of the cliff, tied one rope to the sack so that the mouth was left open, tied the other to Eb, and lowered him and the sack to the ledge. Experienced at this ploy, young Eb handled the affair slowly. The yow was scared, wild of eye. Eb got his back against the wall of rock, bided his time. An immediate attempt might have ended in the yow knocking him over the edge. Presently, the yow less suspicious, he grabbed it, got its hind legs into the sack, shoved its body well down, tied it roughly around the neck, and shouted to them to haul up.

The sheep saved, he glanced about and decided that instead of an awkward haul up for himself, it would be easier to descend. A stunted but strong little rowan was growing out of the rock. If they dropped the other end of the rope to him, he could form a type of sliding loop with it, hook this over the rowan, and lower himself to the head of a steep tilt about 35 feet below. All went well until he was about 15 feet beneath the rowan, descending hand over hand. Looking up, he saw the loop slip off, fell head downwards, twisted himself upright with a convulsive effort, and struck the rocks half-way down the tilt. He broke his left thigh. But, as he said: 'Yow were worth two pun ten.'

Being heaf-bred, sheep never lose themselves in a literal sense, but they may well join another flock on the heights, to be gathered later by a neighbour and returned to the owner direct, or carted along to the next Shepherds' Meet.

The stealing of sheep is a strange, difficult, delicate matter, talked

of in whispers. The late W. T. Palmer wrote an account of an ancient shepherd's experience in the days when the penalty for sheep-stealing was hanging. Night after night yows were disappearing, despite the watching parties organized by the dalesmen. What bewildered them was how sheep could be taken away without trace. Everything travelling by road was checked, and the fell-routes were kept under observation. In the end two young shepherds, puzzled by blaring they failed to locate, climbed what was considered to be an impossible gully. A branch of it, they discovered, forked more gently towards a natural rock platform. Three sides of the platform were walled by the curve of the buttress. The fourth side had been built up artificially with boulders. Stolen sheep were inside this secret fold. The Night Shepherds, as the thieves were called, local men who in fact knew all the plans and time-tables of the watchers, kept their living loot here and fed them, hauling them out with ropes and driving them across the moor during the periods when no watchers were on duty.

On the open, unfenced fell, trust is vital, inevitable. Shepherds and farmers rightly have full faith in one another, help their neighbours, and join in the pleasant tradition of giving boon days. But once in a while somebody breaks the code, and a rustle of unease stirs through the dale. Folk talk about it in guarded fashion. Names remain unmentioned, but we think we know the suspect, and take certain precautions. Logically, the thief must be local. Nobody else could find his way around on fells where visitors lose themselves in broad daylight. And the odds being that he moves by night, then indeed he must be one of us.

Bring in the police? What can a policeman do? The youngest, and most country-bred may know the fells reasonably well. But if he walks about on them, the thief will take warning.

Of several cases known to me, the strangest occurred some ten years ago. A man I knew well, in a neighbouring dale, had lost a lot of sheep. He had his suspicions, and seemed unwilling to voice them. Aware that I was often aloft, he asked me to keep an alert eye open. One summer I crossed a wide moor after midnight. I was driving west, and a brisk breeze blew from that direction. The road bent sharply around a flanking, rocky hummock. Somebody I knew loomed up in the headlights. Fifty yards away a couple of dozen sheep, not his, were being steered along by his dog. He had a whistle, doubtless the high frequency type inaudible to the human ear.

By a sheer fluke, about a fortnight later, I heard of some Herdwick sheep being sold at a Midland auction, an almost unthinkable event down there. When I told all I knew to my friend, expecting him to act, he shook his head sombrely.

'Nay,' he said, 'nay. It 'ud nivver do. It 'ud make us gey bad neighbours.'

I believe that these infrequent cases of sheep-stealing originate from the culprit being hard up, not from a planned career of wickedness. Some young chap with a small, unprofitable farm thinks he sees a way of getting out of his difficulties. If an intelligent dalesman, brought up in the ways of sheep, deliberately chose the stealing of them as a full-time job, he could be a menace to the Lake District. Operating on the open fells in the middle of the night with a well-trained dog and a three-tiered truck, he could present a big problem. He would need some place where the fleeces, with their tell-tale smit marks, could be clipped off in secrecy, and a distant black market.

Sheep away up the fell are vulnerable to another fortunately rare danger, the killer dog. The true sheepdog was developed from a strain that once hunted sheep, and a sudden, inexplicable lapse converts it back to a killer. A few years ago we were puzzled by an outbreak of sheep-worrying on the local fells. Some of the victims were found injured, some dead, and every wound indicated an attack by a dog. Our fells are so far away from a built-up area, worrying by a town dog seemed out of the question. So it meant the worst of all enemies, a lapsed sheepdog.

Farmers and shepherds kept watch, without a clue. Weeks went past, and then three farmers, coming home over the moor one moonlit midnight after a lively evening, saw a few yows scuttling in fright around a heathery hummock. Slowing down the car and staring, they saw a dog loping behind the sheep, and recognized it by its unusual patches of white among the black coat. It belonged to a friend of theirs.

In the morning they told him the shocking news. He refused to believe it. Not only was Nell first-class with sheep, and gentle at that: she was shut in a hull at night, with no chance of getting out.

The three said unhappily: ''Twas Nell. Nay doot at all. Thou watch her.'

Nell's owner watched, and discovered that she had learned the trick of jumping up against the hull door and lifting the sneck. With even greater cunning, on her return into the hull she jumped up at the door, thrusting her muzzle at the sneck so that it fell back into the socket, and thus leaving no evidence that she had been out. Nell had to be shot.

As for the forestry around Bassenthwaite and Derwentwater, a deal of it dates from the unimaginative days of straight lines and straight edges, conifers, conifers everywhere, nor any hardwood to relieve the monotony. Since then the outlook on planting has altered so much, there are places where trees have improved the view. There are thousands of pleasant, sentimental folk who deplore the cutting down of any tree, forgetting that trees, like human beings, grow past their best, become old, and have to die. Pines and their cousins have a comparatively short life, while an oak, I gather, takes 150 years before becoming entitled to the key of the door.

In less than 20 years the methods of woodsmen have speeded up astonishingly. We had a spinney ready for cutting, and two young woodsmen, Bill and Josh, were the surgeons. They stayed with us a month. Bill cared to prove his precision by clapping down his hand on the flat stump of a tree, his fingers and thumb splayed, and bringing his axe down quickly, thud, thud, thud, thud between the digits. Josh would swing his axe and split a match lengthwise. No powered saws for those two, nay. Every morning they went up with their double-handed saw and axes and steel wedges and hammers. The saw bit in for a while, and then the wedge was inserted, and after a few ringing blows, the tree dropped with its bushy head plumping straight into the fragrant fire.

I had to laugh at their apparent contempt for danger. Josh would be tending the fire, and Bill thumping away at the wedge biting into a tall larch. The larch swayed a little: a splitting creak: a swift

rallentundo of splitting as the tree dropped in death. Bill never cried:
'Timber!' Josh never bothered to turn his head. The tree came down
whoomp, its head within feet of him. Those two young men knew
each other's skills.

Not that they never had an accident. Bill, I noticed, suffered from
a slight limp. When I asked him the cause of it he grinned and said:
'Yan o' you feckless fell-farmers. Aye, fair daft.'

He went on to illustrate his point. A gap had developed in the
wall on the fringe of the spinney, and as a temporary repair we had
filled it with rabbit-wire, nailing one end of the wire to a nearby
spruce.

Bill shook a rebuking head. 'Ah'll wager when wire's took away
and wall's built oop, thou'll fergit to pull oot nail.'

I began to see what he was getting at. In the course of years a tree
will grow clean over a nail embedded in it. That was how he had
come to grief, plying his axe on a tree that hid a thick six-inch nail.
The blade glanced off, swept back, and although he leapt desperately,
the steel bit across his ankle bone.

Josh's only accident had been a well-nigh fantastic episode. A
tremendous gale damaged a sizeable tract of woodland across the
Border. The mess had to be cleared up, and it was difficult, trees
sprawled over one another, their branches intertwined. He and his
mate were working on one giant ash that lay prone, its massed,
earthy roots out of the ground and below them the large hole from
which they had been wrenched. Across the trunk of the ash pressed
the branches of another fallen tree, and the two young men were
severing these before they could get at the ash.

Josh, having a rest and a quiet pipe, was standing by the massed
roots. Neither he nor his mate had noticed that one root, thick as a
man's thigh and stretched like a giant spring, extended unbroken
into the ground. As his mate continued to lop the branches of the
other tree, lessening the downward pressure, the ash reacted to the
powerful pull of the root, and swung up. All Josh could do was to
leap into the hole.

Woodsmen seem to wait deliberately for wet weather to haul
away their trees. For months the felled timber lay on the steep fell-

breast, until, in a phase of downpours that turned the surface to a treacherous slide, Josh and Bill, and a very old, nameless, leathery man appeared with a truck, a three-legs, and a crawler. The old man and the crawler were the same colour, and after a while I grew convinced that they were the two parts of an entity, a Crawler-Centaur. They went up the most deadly gradients, chained the fallen trees, snaked and slithered down drawing loads that skidded after them at such slime-induced speed, I could have sworn they would be overtaken and battered and squashed. But always, always Crawler-Centaur reached the flat meadow at the bottom first, and with a swish of his tail, brought the trees sliding safely to one side.

After those performances I could believe anything of him. When the three-legs was erected for the purpose of loading the timber truck, C-C manoeuvred to the precise inch. And when Bill and Josh cruised jauntily down the dale road, with its curves and its stone walls stressing the narrowness, and their loads of long trees swayed sideways and up and down and at the last, breath-taking moment, invariably avoided contact by one inch, I ceased wondering and marvelling from sheer surfeit.

Last year we had another session of professional felling. This time the woodsmen used powered saws. Again one man tended the fire, stooping over its resinous fragrance and paying divine disregard to the falling trees. He and his mate would slice the branches off a prone giant as quickly as the unskilled could trim a hedgerow stick. The crawler had a young master instead of an ancient one, a lad with fair hair, kind blue eyes, and such mastery of his steed as to play a form of tag with the trees he was hauling. There was one accident. He happened to be on the ground instead of on the crawler, and a falling tree hit a large boulder, and whirled around in striking the fell-breast. The cut end of it took him across the back of the hand.

The first I knew of it was a fumbling at the kitchen door. I opened it. Blood was running off the handle and down the woodwork. He lifted a gory mess and said: 'Hesta got a bit o' summat to wrap roond this?'

Washing it under the kitchen tap revealed a deep red groove with a black chunk jammed in the rawness. He rejected the suggestion that he needed a doctor.

'If thou'll pull yon oot—' he said affably.

I pulled it oot, a bit of tree, washed the wound again, and then applied a dressing and a bandage. Five minutes later he was back on the crawler. Next day I inquired after the injury. 'Doin' gey well,' he said, and stuck out his hand. It was so black with honest toil, even the bandage had become invisible.

This unselfconscious toughness, typical of the Lakelander, may stem from living in a tough land. It may have given rise to that old story, possibly a fable, deserving repetition because it highlights the dour commonsense of the Cumbrian. It concerns an old farmer lying very ill upstairs, whose wife at last sent for their married daughter. The girl arrived, went up to the bedroom, and found him unconscious.

'Feyther,' she begged, 'feyther, say summat.'

There was no reaction. Again and again she implored him to speak. At last he stirred and murmured, and the relieved daughter said: 'Oh, feyther, thou maun git better. Ah'll wager thou will. But thou maun eat summat. What 'ud thou like?'

His head shook faintly. Again she pressed him, and again, and at last he muttered: 'Ah, weel, a laal bit o' thin ham.'

Out to the head of the staircase hurried the daughter and called down: 'Moother, moother, feyther could do wi' a laal bit o' thin ham.'

Mother called up firmly: 'If thy feyther thinks ah's gaan to cut intil yon ham before funeral, he can think again.'

Those motoring along by Bassenthwaite, or walking through Borrowdale, or ascending some steepish trod for the masochistic delights of it, should give a thought to the forester who planted all those trees up all those breathless and knotty tilts. There were the saplings and the implements to carry aloft. Thirty years ago and more nearly everything was achieved by the sweat of the brow. Two great alleviators are at their service now, the helicopter and the cellophane bag.

A still and sticky morning once saw me struggling up the Ennerdale flank of Buttermere Red Pike. My companion was new to it, and I grabbed the chance to keep stopping and pointing out various scenes, not really for the benefit of his eyes but for my lungs. A waffling, humming noise disturbed the summer air. It was a helicopter carting up stakes and wire to the spine of a ridge about a thousand feet high on the other side of the dale. I have no doubt that sensible foresters there ascended to work by this same means. With the absurdity of human contradiction I wished I could have a helicopter to tackle Red Pike, or else a chair-lift. Had they been available, I expect I should have turned a contemptuous back on them.

The weary job of temporarily planting out young saplings has been eliminated by the cellophane bag. Put the sapling in the bag, and it creates its own moisture via sweat. I saw a dignified and senior official of the Forestry Commission pat a pile of these bags and say : 'Bless you !'

One other boon has been a type of tractor that tackles marshland, formerly a nightmare to the forester. The machine is so constructed that it can keep going over an actual swamp, cutting a drainage channel as it moves, and gradually getting the ground dry enough for planting. Foulshaw Moss, near Kendal, was conquered this way.

I would like to cruise in a helicopter all over the Lake District, spying out the new plantations as well as the old. Subsidies have encouraged farmers to grow their own timber. With men from the Commission advising them and carrying out the planting, the fell farmer rightly reckons himself lucky. As a legacy, this form of enterprise grows popular with both older and younger generations, there being no liability for death duties until the trees have been cut down.

Travelling north out of Keswick by the road to Penrith, the higher fells stand not only treeless but splendidly bare and forbidding. The expression may sound curious, and yet the combination of the tall and steep and barren does produce a spiritual sense of awe. Up here, on the way to Mungrisdale and beyond the frown of Saddleback, glowers a tarn that disturbed the ancients and made our forbears talk and write solemnly of it. Bowscale Tarn lies so deep below its surrounding rock, even on a fine midday the stars could be seen reflected in its waters. So claimed folk of the past. I have never seen this effect, or met anybody who has, but it would be a pity to dub the story as rubbish. These fells up here, rolling and tumbling and rearing up again all along to Back of Skiddaw have a character that takes a lone walker by the elbow and charges him to be respectful. I have met unknown discomfort on high, honest fear of the dizzy, and a sense of brooding aloneness, but the feeling here is something else. Only in one other place have I met it, on Slieve Gullion, just inside the boundary of Northern Ireland.

Beyond Bowscale and the Caldbeck fells where John Peel earned immortality because of the song—supporters of Tommie Dobson and Bowman declaring their favourites to be better men—Hesket Newmarket abides beyond the hurry and worry of the world. On Saturday mornings, I was told there, the place had some noise, for a few bairns played on the green. Its grey stone houses and emerald fell-breasts and shadowy course of the Caldew do seem to tell you in a whisper that noise here would be sacrilege. A couple of miles further on John Peel has his tomb in Caldbeck churchyard, and the village houses smile here and there, silvery-grey, inconsequent, as if planted by a good-humoured fairy who had no respect for planning.

Returning to the main Keswick-Ambleside road, there lies ahead Manchester's dubious triumph, Thirlmere, wooded and barred from public enjoyment. By road, both sides have their charm, though the main route suffers from traffic. Thirlmere in itself is a lake of distinction, and in recent years the weight of public opinion has cracked some of the Mancunian interdicts. But to give it a harsh name, it is still a Manchester reservoir.

CHAPTER NINE

November

Out of Ambleside, heading for Kirkstone and Ullswater, clambers a road called the Struggle. Horses must have found it merciless. To a reasonable car with a kind driver it is simply a major climb. To any-body travelling from the south on a day's visit to Ullswater the most revealing way there is via Troutbeck. Return by the Struggle; the world below keeps unfolding like some gigantic map.

Despite the main road, Kirkstone Pass itself can be grim and deso-late in grey weather. Always in my mind will it remain the place where tragedy came to many. Two coach-loads of holidaymakers were involved, and some of them, heavily bandaged, later gave evi-dence at the Coroner's Inquest, where I was one of a jury of nine. The coaches belonged to a small firm. They were about 200 yards apart when the second coach failed; both handbrake and footbrake refused to work; the driver fought to hold it in gear, but it jumped out, and there they were, tearing downhill, the coach swivelling like a silverfish as the driver evaded three private cars coming up and two going down. Desperate, he steered for the coach in front, hoping and praying to check his speed without excessive harm to his own or the other. In his mirror the driver ahead caught sight of the approaching threat. He tried to dodge, but had no chance.

The flanking fells are bleak and steep, and inviting to adventurous feet. Even the timid and breathless could gain enjoyment by using a simple method. Take 50 paces, or only 25, and halt for half a minute. The tallest fells can be captured by gentle guile. Another technique, more difficult, though immensely effective when once achieved, is to have a row with your companion. You forget the physical effort in searching for destructive argument, and the output of adrenalin has a jet-propelling influence.

The argument may be allowed to subside in Patterdale, with its peaceful ease and good humour. Here you can laugh at the discomfiture of the insurance agent who was trying to persuade a local farmer to take out a fire policy. Pouring out a cascade of sales talk he went on and on, getting more and more confident that his potential and silent customer would be convinced to the hilt. At last he paused for breath. Then the farmer opened his mouth.

'Nay,' he said slowly. 'We don't need yan (one) o' them. We've nivver hed a fire.'

Ullswater is worth seeing in two completely differing ways, from its banks and from its breast. The chief road keeps to the western shores wherever it can, past the amusing conceit of Lyulph's Tower, and the track to Aira Force, a waterfall over-visited in summer, but not to be despised; the path attending it leads to higher things. The three great reaches of the lake, translated into music, would be chords played respectively by Wagner, Chopin and Schubert, whether viewed from the western or eastern shore; this latter has a road to Sharrow Bay and How Tarn. Thence feet do better than wheels, and red deer better than both.

Well along the western road branching off to Penruddock smiles the mellow old house of Hutton John, lived in by descendants of the Huddlestones of Millom. And not far from Hutton John is another house, at Wreay, which from a distance looks like a hamlet. It provided a woman friend of mine with a startling experience. She was asked to act as companion for a fortnight to the elderly owner, the regular companion having to enter hospital. Knowing nothing of the circumstances, the deputy agreed, only to discover that the house was large, with about two dozen bedrooms under dust covers, and no staff. The owner, in her nineties, expected the companion to dress her for dinner, cook the dinner, serve it, and also sit at table. Dickens himself could hardly have created a more odd situation. One morning, taking tea to the old lady, the companion found the bed empty. Faint sounds led her to look beneath. She was lying under the bed, having fallen out in the night and become too exhausted to move or shout for help.

Pooley Bridge might be called the port of Ullswater. Its annual sports were famous, if only for the attendance of Lordie. To the southerner this may convey nothing. To folk of the Ullswater area the name of Lordie is yet a nostalgic talisman. The great Lord Lonsdale, cock of the North-West, sitting in his black and yellow carriage drawn by shining horses, probably meant more to the crowd than anybody else in the world. An elderly Patterdale farmer assured me that the rumbling sound of the wheels on the turf, and the creaking of leather and the gleaming of the silver-mounted harness roused folk to a kind of triumphant delight.

Come with me to what is left of his castle. Out of Pooley Bridge, turn right for Askham, where in the creamy-pink dower house lives the present Earl, a scientific farmer who has fashioned the huge estates into models of agriculture. Cross the bridge, into the park, and stare for a while at the long, pale façade, a memorial to Hugh Lowther, most powerful, most picturesque, most flamboyant of the Lonsdale Earls. His castle, rebuilt in the early 1800's, was too hopelessly large for modern living, and so his successors dismantled it, leaving the façade as an imaginative gesture to posterity. Nobody need deplore the loss of the building itself. I was in it once, and the grandeur seemed ugly, uncomfortable, despite the fact that Lordie took especial pains to give it luxury during the stay of an important guest, Kaiser William. The pains included the electrical heating of the lavatory seats. Later, rumour had it that the Kaiser intended to make the castle his northern headquarters when he conquered England. Maybe his incentive was the warm personal touch.

Lordie belonged to a unique generation. The youngest and last of them was Winston Churchill. They were tough in mind, tough in body, dominant, brimming with leadership. Beside them, petty politicians and academic theorists seem futile. Apart from his general support of boxing and the Turf, there were Lordie's own fantastic achievements. In America he fought three exhibition rounds with the World Heavyweight Champion. In the second round the Champion, losing his temper under Lordie's brisk hammering, turned the contest into a fight. Only too ready to oblige, Lordie knocked him out stone cold.

There was the One Hundred Miles Walking Contest, between Knightsbridge Barracks and the Ramjam Inn on the Great North Road. The World's Walking Champion, again an American, was backed by the fancy for large sums. Lordie, then only the Hon. Hugh Lowther, had a sporting peer to sponsor him. He left the American standing, beating him by ten miles. No wonder the folk of the Lake District, and the people of England, cheered with genuine affection when they caught sight of his red face and his large cigar. Men of his ilk make a country great, and are hailed by all except the bleating and jealous nonentities.

Lordie's land agent had a son who entered the navy, and from him I heard some rich stories about his father's boss. There was the instant and wholesale surge of Lonsdale patriotism on the outbreak of the first War. He enlisted a battalion of his tenants and their friends, provided them with uniform, and appointed his own officers. Unorthodox, illegal, generous, the gesture had to be given kid-glove treatment by the War Office. The battalion was quietly incorporated into the Army. There was the account of his daily, personal routine. A valet awoke him in the morning with a cigar and a double brandy. Is it possible that had he preferred tea instead, he would have been beaten by the American champion?

'As for common sense,' said the naval officer, 'he had heaps.' Accompanied by his agent, driving in a trap and inspecting part of his estate, Lordie had drawn up for lunch at a Westmorland inn. The two ate well and drank well. The afternoon was chilly, and about three o'clock Lordie stopped the trap and walked across to a hedge. The agent, joining him, happened to glance to the left, and said hurriedly: 'Milord! there's a woman coming along.'

'What of it?' said Lordie. 'If she's a lady, she won't look, and if she isn't, it doesn't matter.'

Before the castle was demolished the sale of the contents went on for many days. Walking through the park, I wondered what would happen to these wide lands. The Forces had been in occupation, and there were derelict car-parks and areas of casual neglect. The flower gardens were sad, and every growing thing somehow reminded me of Tosti's melancholy farewell, 'Goodbye, Summer.' Little did any of us reckon that new life would spring up, the robust and heartening life of good farming.

As I wandered, slowly and quietly, along a path screened by shrubs, I caught a glimpse of two figures beyond the leaves. They were youngish women, well-dressed in tweeds. One was stooping, a trowel in her hand. The other stood alert and watchful, keeping 'Cave'. Pretending not to have noticed anything, I sauntered into the open. They assumed a smiling innocence and said: 'Good morning.' I wish the ghost of Lordie could have been there. He would have bellowed with laughter and invited them in for a drink. Had they been men he would have knocked them down and then plied them with whisky.

Every item that came up for sale drew eager bids. What I coveted most were the horse-drawn vehicles in the Lonsdale colours, black and yellow. One, a small, covered carriage, romantically ideal for elopement, made me itch to possess it. In perfect condition, the work of craftsmen, it deserved to be in some museum of beautiful skills. I stepped inside, sat down. The leather creaked faintly, and the fragrance of it conjured up a bonnet and curls and fur and high-waisted silks. A nasty little practical imp sneered in my ear: 'Don't be daft. What can you do with the thing? Buy a horse and drive it up and down the dale road?'

The lot went to Sir Alexander Korda, for use in period films.

One or two other lots led to surprises. A painting for which a knowledgeable dealer paid a hundred pounds sold subsequently for tens of thousands. A friend of mine, driven to giving up tobacco by his doctor, and taking to snuff as a consolation, was wandering around Caledonian Market and saw a well-made but filthy little box. The stall-owner asked a pound for it. After innumerable immersions and scrubbings it proved to be a silver snuff-box, with the Lowther arms set in gems.

Another place, nearby, was lost to the world a decade before Lowther Castle, when Manchester Corporation drowned Mardale, to form their Haweswater reservoir. Approaching from Bampton, anyone unaware of the story would accept the stretch of water as a natural lake faced by a man-made barrage at the lower end. But one dry year, during an exceptional drought, a bit of Mardale Church was visible. I know a not-so-elderly couple who spent their honeymoon at the Dun Bull in Mardale. Some 20 years ago I went with them to Haweswater. We drove slowly along the flanking road. Then he parked the car, and as we idled, he and his wife grew reminiscent.

'It must have been there where we watched that gorgeous sunset.' His finger pointed at water.

'Yes. And d'you remember that afternoon when we had a picnic and the flies were so bad?' Her slimmer finger pointed at water. 'There, d'you think?'

'Or was it there?'

'And that day I twisted my ankle and you carried me. About there?'

'Yes, dear. About there.' They stared, and sighed, and stared again, right into the middle of the lake.

With packets of sandwiches we walked slowly up to Riggindale Crags, nibbled, dozed a little, descended diagonally for a while, sat down again. Some way below us was Blea Water, the surface dappled by rising trout. As an angling addict, he groaned aloud at having no rod. So I tried to distract him by nodding towards High Street and marvelling how the Romans could have constructed a way over that tall fell.

'D'you know,' said his wife, 'on our honeymoon he never fished once. That was the greatest compliment I've ever been paid.'

I laughed and nodded, and recalled how only two days ago I had been with him by another fell tarn. There he had all his tackle, and conditions, for the middle of May, were ideal, a sunny sky, a lively breeze, the fish hungry, and the first break of fly. At the end of the afternoon he wanted to know where he could hire a tent. When I asked him what for, he said: 'To stay up here.' His wife? Oh, she would be all right in the hotel.

Like the rest of the fells, these about Haweswater provide a living for sheep above and cattle below. In some of the intakes will be tups, chained together by the horns and wandering moodily, their breeding instincts expressed in outbursts of growling. More than one town visitor, strolling peacefully along a dale lane in November, has nearly jumped out of a startled skin at a sudden tigerish snarl. Breeding time varies from flock to flock, according to its nearness to the high fell. But at some phase during this month most of the yows will be brought down. Like humans, there are flirts among them. One of the most reprehensible ovine performances I ever saw concerned a pair of tups, chained, on one side of a strong wire fence; on the other was a flirtatious yow. She taunted them, whickered, wriggled, brushed herself against the wire and gave them a sort of come-hither tilt of the head. Growling savagely, each tup nuzzled her. As each made the attempt, the other butted him away. The yow was having a lovely time.

After the mating, when one tup may serve 50 wives, the yows go back to the fell, but the more valuable and therefore pampered husbands are kept below in comfort. More than once, in an apologetic whisper, I have been asked how we know that mating has taken place. The answer is ridiculously simple. The tup is smeared with smit, and if any yow shows no sign of being marked by it, we conclude that she is yet to be wed. Once we had a tup of such discernment, he was kept in attendance while the yows filed past up the fell. He knew at once if any had escaped attention, and remedied the omission.

As for the beasts, they will still be out if November is reasonably gentle. Once really hard frost has killed the grazing, most breeds have to be inside, and the expenses start, hay and cake to be fed to them, perhaps until late in the following May. I have no statistics by me concerning the diverse breeds in Lakeland, but Friesians, Galloways and Herefords will be a lot in evidence. Until after the last War farms in the upper dales ran Shorthorns, and not many of those. Friesians were described contemptuously as walking water barrels. Scientific methods increased their standard. Next, the accent swung from milk to meat, and the heavier Friesian offered larger profit. After that somebody pointed out that a beast fit to stay on the fell all winter would be welcome, and thus the shaggy Galloway came into its own. Shaggy it is, almost frowsty compared with the sleeker breeds. But its near cousin, the Beltie, has a touch of the fashion model. On a hillside on the way to Castle Douglas a Beltie herd positively flaunts its black and white elegance. I have wished before and wish again that some artist would paint a picture of black and white Friesians or Belties, escorted by black and white sheepdogs, with magpies overhead.

The most recent favourite, the Hereford crossed with the Galloway, spends a drowsy, comfortable day and night on the cold winter fell. Even the bull looks benign, though no bull should ever be trusted by a stranger. If it comes to that, the occasional cow can be unladylike. There may be provocation, of course. One of ours, in a rubbing mood, lifted a gate off its hinges. Bewildered and indignant she charged about the meadow, faintly suggesting Shakespeare's words 'till Birnam Wood do come to Dunsinane'. Removing the gate was no light matter.

Another cow fell temporary victim to somebody's shameful carelessness. A length of strong wire, looped at one end, had been left in a pasture. My first knowledge of it was when I saw a cow acting strangely. The loop was around her horns. The wire stretched down, under her belly, and had wrapped itself tightly about her off hind leg. Every time she moved, her head was jerked down. Several wary attempts of mine failed, and she was growing dangerous. I tried a last effort, and the loop suddenly came free. She gave no bother, bless her, while I unwound the wire from her leg.

Mention the name of Shap to any experienced northern lorry-driver, and his eyes would flash and his tongue utter fire. Small blame to him. The winds and the snows on the road over Shap Fell brought blockades without number. Part of its wickedness is the absence of any screening. Fells that pile up neck-breaking crags and brutal barriers at least have the merit of obstructing a gale. Shap, with no such protection, seemed to specialize in paralysing traffic. There was compiled a list of folk in Shap village willing to put up drivers whose vehicles were stuck on the pass. To any driver who at last achieved escape from this white and wind-swept wilderness, his entry into the calm of Penrith must have seemed like a protecting harbour after a violent Atlantic passage.

Machines chug and hack and scrape and delve as the new road

unrolls itself, yellowish and raw, avoiding the worst of Shap and promising a hopeful journey in ugly weather. The farming community along here is being robbed of fruitful acres. For once, I think few of us deplore the loss. Shap had an evil name, and since the life of the country now depends on transport, fields must be sacrificed to satisfy the hunger for negotiable roads.

Here is a run of country the Romans knew well, and the machines that dig and scoop are turning up mementoes of Roman life 1,800 years ago and more. By arrangement with the Ministry of Transport, all the finds are supposed to be handed over to the Ministry of Works. To expect the men to stick to this rule rigidly is asking a lot of human nature. At any rate, a fair selection of antiquarian interest has been passed over, providing an exhibition ranging from jewellery to weapons. In the end the new way across Shap may prove gentler than the train journey. My first rail ride from Kendal to Penrith was a near-nightmare, thundering and swaying down the steep gradient, rain smothering the windows with semi-blind cascades, trees bending and flailing themselves wildly, and the ravine far below seeming to wait for us to heel over and pitch off the line. With a sort of shaky determination I chose a long word in the newspaper on my lap and bet myself I could make 40 words out of it. I stuck at 33, and was still cudgelling my brain for more when we slid to a halt in the haven of Penrith.

The churchyard, with its Giant's grave and precincts, was soothing after the train journey. Next, the Beacon above the town drew me up the hill to it. It must have flared its warning at the time of the Armada, when, not so far off, 'the red glare on Skiddaw roused the burghers of Carlisle'. Perhaps it flared again in the anxious years of the '15 and the '45.

Penrith's most exciting days since then centre around traffic jams. At the bottle-neck in the middle of the town I have seen a bulging lorry protrude over the slip of pavement and nudge a little girl flat without hurting her. I have seen drivers and police and pedestrians all verging on good-humoured insanity. I have talked to local folk who told me that the problem had been under discussion for 30 years and more. I have believed that for its long suffering and

25 *Kirkstone Pass, looking towards Brothers Water*

patience the British public deserved to be canonized. And once, in desperation, I dared to take on traffic control for a space.

The time was between four and five o'clock. Three of us had driven in from Pooley Bridge, parked the car, crossed the main road and gone up to post some letters in a box in a side road. When we turned back the policeman on duty had vanished, and the north- and south-bound traffic rattled and snorted and rolled past in a manner reminiscent of that hymn line 'Time like an everlasting stream—'. Pedestrians were gathering, thicker and thicker, school-children, women shoppers, men young and old, and soon the pavements could scarcely hold the press of them. No faintest sign of a break showed in the traffic. A very large van, slightly slower than the mainstream, was approaching us. Annoyance and a flaring lust for tea nudged me into the road. I smiled at the driver, held up my hand, and received a jovial grin in reply. He stopped, and for something like a minute people surged across. The bye-pass, I suppose, will eliminate such incidents. I am not quite sure if I shall prefer a safe and organized Penrith.

Carlisle, its larger and distinguished neighbour, invented a positively thrilling traffic game. In a bus coming up from Penrith, and entering the tight congestion of Botcherby, I had to juggle with a tricky problem. My train was due out of the station in ten minutes. From where I sat in the stationary bus with a heavy suit-case I might, half-walking, half-trotting, get to the station in nine minutes. If the bus proceeded at its present rate, it would reach the station in eleven minutes. The conductor wished me luck. I stepped off, glanced back later as I diverted into the station yard to see the bus marooned quite a way off, and caught the train by seconds.

Another game, created by an adjustment of routes, involved both English Street and Lowther Street, heaps of traffic signs, and sandstone islands. I sat on the first floor of a café and stared out, enchanted by the scene. Huge vehicles from Scotland were clawing their way around a narrow bend and down a residential road. Residents were staring through their threatened windows and then turning away in dread. It would be unfair to blame the present. The past should have taken action a full generation ago.

Carlisle, its first syllable stressed by Cumbrians, is a mixture of antiquity, chimneyed industry, and green space. The Castle with its ramparts and its curving terrace summons up a thrilling and bloody history. In the far past the Romans gave Carlisle a place in the sun. Those Roman times come back to life in Tullie House, close by the Cathedral, where ancient reality brings 'then' very close to 'now'. The Scots destroyed the town, left it a flat clutter of stones. William Rufus, tactically shrewd, gave the authority for rebuilding. West Walls, behind the Cathedral precincts and loftily abutting on the railway, still boast courses of sandstone blocks that were placed there in 1087. Walk below them, and touch them, and think of the hands that put them into position. History lives in Carlisle, not simply dull words.

History, some of it sad and dreadful, went on living vividly there through the '15 and the '45. Few men of the Lake District proper took active part in these risings. But some on the fringes joined Charles Edward, and paid tragic penalty. In black-hole-of-Calcutta conditions about 90 of them awaited their trial in the Castle. Most suffered the horrible details of hanging, drawing and quartering on Harraby Hill, now the home of a modern trading Estate and Border Television. According to a contemporary account they were calm and un-hating to the end.

As if to counter-balance the jostle of the traffic, the city has narrow lanes linking the big streets, lanes of yesterday, quiet, un-obtrusive, with small shops here and there. May they remain un-changed in their demure invitation. If you prefer something wider, there is the covered market. It sells almost anything, in a leisurely, friendly manner. Anybody disliking harsh weather could stroll around under this ample roof, enjoying exercise, human interest, shop-gazing, for a whole morning at no cost.

What of sauntering in fine weather? The answer in Carlisle is a surprise. From the shopping centre of the city a stroll of ten minutes brings you to open country, where the wide Eden, fed by the Caldew and the Petteril, slides and gushes and sparkles between banks flushed pink by wild flowers in the coloured season. Over the bridge linking south with north throbs endless traffic. But on either side spreads the greenery, on and on, and you can idle among it, and imagine yourself miles away. Rickerby park, on the north side, approaches so near, I vow that no city in the world can boast such imminence of the rural.

Repeating that almost silly question, where does the Lake District end? I would suggest that anybody with a car, or the price of a bus fare, or active legs, should refuse to be limited by a dotted line on a map. Brampton, ten miles from Carlisle, provides nearby a dramatic introduction to the Roman Wall. I watched the Ministry of Works men dealing with a recently uncovered section, and smiled at the casual and not quite proper scratchings in the stone left behind by bored legionaries. Brampton inevitably leads to Naworth Castle, where the Howards dealt out justice in the wild days of the Border. The greatest of them, Belted Will, was orphaned at the age of nine, when they executed his father, Thomas, Duke of Norfolk.

The love between Will and his wife is a story of classic quality. At 14 he was wed to Lady Elizabeth Dacre, a few months younger than the boy. Unjustly imprisoned and heavily fined, he regained his estate under James the First. Raiders reckoned him stern and fierce. Honest folk acclaimed him as 'the Civilizer of our Borders'. On his various missions he never forgot to send adoring messages to his wife. Stern he was with evil-doers, and stern with himself, for so mulcted had he been by Queen Elizabeth, he denied himself any personal luxury. In 1619 he allowed himself 20/- per month, and by 1627 he had raised it to the modest figure of £36 per year. His accounts were meticulous. 'A black frieze jerkin, 16 shillings; silk hose, 36 shillings; two pairs of spectacles, at 18 pence per pair.' Presents to his wife included a watch costing four pounds, a 'somer' gown at six pounds, and two fine felt hats at seven shillings apiece.

When they had been married 60 years, and she was 73, he had their portraits painted by Jansen, and copies of them are now at Naworth. The clothing he wears in the picture is described as— 'a close jacket of figured thick silk with rounded skirts to mid-thigh, and many small buttons: hose of black silk, tied with silk garters and bows; a plain falling shirt collar, sleeves turned up at the wrist; dress rapier with a gilt basket-hilt hanging by a narrow belt of black velvet with gilt hooks; the cost of all, £17 17s. 6d.'

Stand below the walls of Naworth and imagine Lord William Howard riding out, and turning to wave back to his lady whom he never stopped worshipping. She died in 1640 and he followed her gladly the next year.

Two centuries and more later another great character reigned at Naworth, Rosalind, Countess of Carlisle. 'Agin' her own kind, she turned all the inns under her jurisdiction into temperance hotels, and they are thus until this day. She spurned the Tories and supported the Liberals. One of her daughters married the celebrated Professor Gilbert Murray, and the other became the wife of the late C. G. Roberts, Chairman of the Cumberland County Council. She carted these two sons-in-law to a meeting of the Liberal party. Addressing the audience, she said: 'You needn't think that because I'm a countess I favour the upper classes. I don't. Both my daughters married working-class men. Get up, you two, and show yourselves.'

One of her grandsons told me how, as a very little boy, he was summoned to Naworth. Grannie sat in state, leaning on a stick, and surrounded by minions. These she dismissed, and then turning to the shy child said brusquely: 'Boy, would you marry for money?'

Not having the faintest idea of what she was talking about, he gulped and hung his head.

'Come on, boy!' she said. 'I don't want to think my grandson's a fool. Answer me.'

Because he could think of nothing else, he stammered: 'N-no, Grannie.'

At that she jerked the red cord of an old-fashioned bell-pull. A footman appeared, and she said: 'Give the boy a pound. He's got some sense.'

A great-granddaughter of hers, who lived in one of the ancient Howard houses, and dismissed all ideas of the supernatural with youthful amusement, mentioned that great-grandma haunted the place. When I said: 'But you've just told me you didn't believe in ghosts,' she answered slowly: 'Well, of course, great-grandma's different.'

By a similar mode of argument I am still wandering near the

Border instead of returning yet inside those dotted lines that try to enclose Lakeland. How can I leave out the sacred neighbour of Naworth, Lanercost Priory? There is enough past glory, and beauty and sadness about Lanercost to embrace a man and hide him for hours from the brash life of today. As for far Bewcastle and its Cross, youngsters boarding at Keswick school still believe that pupils from Bewcastle are foreigners. Could there be any greater tribute to the unspoilt than that?

A year before the development of the rocket range I tramped with a friend across Spadeadam Waste, on a walking tour with a tape-recorder, at the instance of the B.B.C. The producer, who was to meet us on the other side at Wark, mentioned too casually that there might be an odd bull somewhere around. He also said that the walk would take no more than three hours.

We met the bull where there was no ditch in which to grovel, no wall to leap, no tree to climb, and the great white beast started to paw the ground. Running would have been madness. We walked with a measured step, holding a painfully polite conversation about old china or glass or something of similar non-violence. The test came when we had passed the creature and dared not look back. It began to mutter and let out preliminary bellows. I care to think that even a matador would have felt squeamish.

Our other inconvenience was a wide and deep drainage channel, unknown to the hopeful producer. With the great expansion of Kielder Forest, the very face of the map had been changed since the producer had walked this way years before. Short of swimming it and ruining the tape-recorder, we had no option but to turn aside and walk and walk and walk.

CHAPTER TEN

December

By December most of the Lake District has reverted to a private
world of its own. A few of the hotels and Youth Hostels may be busy
over Christmas. Meanwhile, solitude returns to the fells and dales.
As for the weather, its variations are beyond guessing. The first week
may be soft, lazy, the lingering larch needles golden under a sun
that warms until mid-afternoon. The roads are deserted and quietude
is dominant, although beneath it weaves a murmur blending the
ripple of a beck, the distant whicker of a sheep, the *pronk* of a
raven, the chugging of a tractor. Hollies, glinting with their harvest
of berries, are still and almost startling against the paleness of the
fields. To us who live among this, town life seems especially remote
as Christmas draws near. Decorated shops, crowded pavements,
processions of cars, traffic lights, these are as far removed as the
stage coaches galloping through the coloured Christmas numbers
of magazines.

Growing lambs are already gone to their wintering on the coast,
or else dotting the dale pastures, and spending their nights under
the sheltering roof of a hoggus, a building usually constructed with
one side open to the weather. The beasts have returned to the byre,
though they get a full stint of outside grazing in the warmth of the
day. Old folk reckon that a crisp October portends a mild December
and quote: 'If October ice will bear a dook (duck), at Christmas
'twill be sloodge and mook.' I think this less reliable than another
belief, about the tiny hanging puffs of cloud often present in wet
weather. They rise and fall like wayward balloons, and the saying

runs: 'Sop (puff) oop, rain doon; sop doon, rain oop.' It seems to work, and presently, with 'sop doon' the becks begin to fall as well.

The time to clean these becks is in early winter or after the spring thaw, though this latter may clash with lambing. Folk used to sluggish streams in the south might think that our fast and frisking becks clean themselves by the very reason of their speed. When thickness shrouds the tops, and the larger becks throb in spate, and the new and temporary spouts of whiteness lace the fell-breasts, it would seem that all this downroar of water must keep the channels flushed and free.

Not so. Spriggy bog-myrtle finds anchorage; seeves, the tubular reeds that provided their pith to make tallow dips, colonize the edges; mosses gum themselves about the roots. In every valley these becks offer natural field drainage, providing the farmer plays his part. The local name of the job is guttering, and includes the removal of dead-tongue, water aconite that will readily kill a beast grazing along the beck edges.

In one of our fields a beck had been diverted a century or so ago, its convenient wrigglings eliminated, and a new, straight course dug and revetted with sizeable stones. Through the passing of time beasts browsing on the frequently soft ground had made the beck narrower, their weight gradually coaxing the soil forwards and downwards so that the revetted walls themselves drew closer together. We decided, well ahead, to carry out a major operation if there should be a mild December. Salmon come to spawn up this beck, their backs projecting like submarines above the shallow water, and with the idea of discouraging them from a waste of spawn, Derwent fixed wire netting at the lower end of the beck.

On a quiet Monday, the sky a greyish yellow and the water low, we started the work. Derwent and I served under Eb's direction, for the old man is a master of stone. There were some wickedly tenacious seeves to extract, their roots tough and deep and defiant. Sharpened spades jabbed and hacked, and then Derwent smacked the tines of the muck-drag hard into the target. To have attempted to pull the offender straight out might have defeated even his youthful strength. He rocked to and fro, and the seeve made wet, gluggy noises. There

was a long-drawn, sucking sigh. A great dripping gobbet of mud and seeve roots detached itself from the bed and was hauled clear.

Next, Derwent lowered himself into the beck to tackle a boulder that would have to be brought into alignment. His muscles grew taut and a vein showed in his temples.

Eb smirked. As an ancient master of stone he employs his own form of magic. He waved Derwent aside, took his place, stooped over the resolute chunk of granite. Then he patted it gently here and there. His lips were moving, probably in some powerful incantation. Anyway, the boulder came up with the ease of a balloon, and the admiring Derwent cried 'By—!'

Despite the wire netting, a hen—and probably a cock-salmon as well—must have got through the barrier, for presently Eb was stooping and scooping gently.

'Look yon,' he said, raising his half-cupped hands.

The thin yellow sunlight shone on a heap of what might have been pinkish pearls. Whether the cock had spread over them his milt we could not be sure. Where Eb found the spawn the gravelly bed of the beck had been hollowed out industriously by the mother-to-be.

Eb sighed, and returned his find to the hollow.

'Aye,' he said. 'Mebbe a gey sad waste. Anyways, them wicked eels might hev got 'em.'

Derwent drew his pipe from his mouth and spat. That was his opinion of eels. Some days earlier, guttering what had been no more than an oozy hollow, we had dispersed 27 eels in a space of 50 yards. Grabbing one by its tail, Derwent had incurred a painful bite from the needle teeth.

In the afternoon, just before tea, Eb jerked his thumb in the direction of the bridge crossing the Esk, into which the beck drains.

'Hesta (have you) been yon sen (since) Friday?'

I shook my head and Derwent said: 'Nay, why?'

'I'll show thee summat.'

We followed him out of the pasture, over the road, and along the lonnin to where a humpback curves with strong elegance to serve two farms on the other side of the river. Immediately downstream of this bridge ponders a pensive pool, smooth, green-gold, only

27 *Askham, near Lowther*

ruffled when a high spate takes command. On our side the naked granite has obliged with a natural if uneven quay. Trees press fairly close; alders, a holly, bird-cherry, a rowan still offering a few berries though no leaves.

The pool is a favourite of spawning salmon, and as we approached cautiously, Eb raised a forbidding hand. We stopped, and his indicating finger jabbed out solemnly.

'Looksta! (look you)' he whispered.

I counted 18 of them. Among the shadowy congregation of unmoving submarines was one facing the platform, its head almost touching the rock.

Eb whispered again. 'Yon's a hen. Ten or eleven poonds, mebbe. Reckon she's spawned a'ready.'

With a gesture he warned us to keep still. I could understand that. Any forward movement might have thrown our shadows over the water. What I could not understand was how he managed to creep along minus his own shadow, like some modern Student of Prague. He crouched on the edge of the platform. The hen salmon stirred not an inch. He stooped, slipped his left hand into the water, closed his fingers and thumb over the root of the tail. The salmon stirred not an inch. He straightened himself, lifted the salmon out of the water, held it at arm's length. For quite five miraculous seconds it remained there as if drowsily enjoying this novel experience. Then it suddenly writhed and thrashed and twisted, and Eb chuckled and tossed it back into the river.

Derwent gaped. 'By—!'

I quite agreed with him.

As December slides on towards its days of celebration the young are hoping understandably for snow or ice or both, ice to coat the lakes and tarns thick enough for skating, snow to provide a ski-run somewhere. This kind of coldness is seasonal, decent, and brings no undue worry to the farmer. The fell sheep are comfortable enough. They can flourish in freezing air for a spell, though a man going aloft to keep an eye on them would be wise to tie a scarf around his ears, or pull a cap well down over them. On a still but stinging December day I ascended Scafell, and too late realized that my left ear was tingling. That frost-bite lingered, in an on-and-off fashion, for a couple of years.

What we dread is the north-west gale that brings cold rain and sleet. Hill sheep, particularly the Herdwick, have a barrier of grease inside their fleece resembling solid brilliantine. What might be termed ordinary vile weather leaves them untroubled. But a tearing nor'-wester lifts the fleece, admitting the driven rain, and the grease is penetrated and the skin grows cold. To counteract this some enterprising sheep-farmers devised a winter jacket, made of sacking treated with a water-proofing agent. Covering the upper part of the sheep from neck to rump, it was intended mainly to prevent the ruffling up of the fleece.

Although the basic pattern of English weather appears to be changing, and places that once believed themselves lucky are now getting disillusioned, I doubt if many folk realize the ferocity of a bad nor'-wester in Lakeland. It will stop a strong man dead in his tracks. As a cross wind it makes normal walking impossible, for at every other attempted stride the lifted foot is blown across the other. Clouds of sullen ebony swirl over the fells, and old heather and brackens and even mosses may be whipped out of the ground.

Days of that kind are days to be spent indoors. Maybe a car load of neighbours arrives in the rain-lashed stack-yard. They make a dash for the big kitchen, and with chairs drawn up on the warm flags and their faces towards the fire, they have a crack about this and that, most of it relating to mutual acquaintances. Stories of quaint characters we know come thick and fast, some of them about a previous sub-mistress of my own dale, Mrs. Martin. A law unto herself, she hoarded her own stamps. My first encounter with her was when I asked for half a dozen tuppenny ones. She said in a rebuking screech: 'Six! what do thou want six for? Nay, thou can hev three.'

Suspicion was her meat and drink. The late Lord Lindsay of Birker, formerly Master of Balliol, had a holiday house not far off, and receiving a postal order for two and ninepence, went to cash it. Not knowing him, Mrs. Martin took the order, stared at him over her spectacles, and retired to a room at the back. He waited and waited, and at last dared to lift the counter-flap and walk through, into a dim room thickened by a bluish-brown fug. Mrs. Martin was still holding the slip of paper and staring at some sort of document pinned to the wall.

He said indignantly: 'Why are you keeping me waiting like this?'

Her stern answer was: 'Ah's lookin' up t'list of stolen postal orders.'

During the War three local girls married service men. The nearest place to draw their separation allowance was at Mrs. Martin's. Rather scared of the old lady, they approached her in a body and explained the position. She drew an aggressive sigh and said:

'H'm. Postmaster thinks ah's a slave, does he? Well, ah's not goin' to kill meself.' Pointing from one to another she declared: 'Thou'll coom on Mondays, thou on Wednesdays, and thou on Fridays.'

Before she knew me, I had a tussle over a copy of the local weekly paper. A neighbour had asked me to collect it, and I dropped in and explained that I was fetching it on behalf of So-and-So.

She shook her head. 'Nay. Don't know thee.'

More explanations were a waste of breath, but at length I half convinced her by fishing out an envelope addressed to me care of So-and-So. Still dubious, she muttered: 'Ah'll risk it,' went into the dim room at the back, and returned, trying to smooth out a badly creased paper. As she handed it over she said: 'Ah oalas (always) reads it first.'

Behind her suspicion was a sense of humour and great love for an old, blind dog.

There was the dale policeman who made Baron Munchhausen seem almost truthful. Planning a holiday in the Isle of Man, he booked passages for his wife and family. Being, according to himself, a good swimmer, he decided to save money by swimming there. Later he told us how the swim had exceeded his calculations. At long last he had stumbled ashore and spoken to a young chap, only to learn he had landed in Ulster. He believed in live and let live, and obligingly tried to keep local folk out of trouble. A lad who had just bought a motor bike was involved in an accident. Our dale policeman took reluctant notes.

'What speed were thou doin'?'

'Two mile an hour.'

'Two mile an hour!'

'Aye.'

Willing as he was, this seemed too much to stomach. He sucked his pencil, considered the lad with a sympathetic but uneasy look, and clutching at compromise, burst out: 'Nay, dammit! say fower.'

There was the elderly farmer who had been celebrating. Temporarily retiring elsewhere with a friend, he mistakenly fixed his cuff-button to himself, and cried in muzzy horror: 'Ah's been seized be (by) stroke! Ah can't move arm!'

A change of weather persuades us to take a day off, combining a run round with a little Christmas shopping. First we head for Appleby, ancient, no larger than a village, Westmorland's toy capital. Certainly the main road from Scotch Corner to the Border, running past the eastern edge, is full of noise and traffic, but Appleby proper has its own life on the other side of the bridge, a handful of shops, cloistered church, a medieval town hall, houses and cottages fronted by lawns and trees, and the Castle at the top of the hill. As for its cricket ground by the Eden, to sit there is to be in the good old England of the past, among the mellowness and kindness and security that once was general and now seems almost lost. Inevitably those last two words recall what happens time and again to a well-swiped cricket ball. It clears the ground and falls into the river. The cricketers keep especial rescue gadgets, and in a minute or so fish out the ball and get on with the game. I feel that the most hidebound Communist would learn a lot if he idled here on a serene afternoon and watched the Appleby cricketers playing for sheer pleasure and no ulterior purpose.

It comes as a queer thought that gentle Appleby's history is stained with violence. After one particularly devastating raid by the Scots it lay a burned and crumbled ruin, a prosperous town put to death by fire and sword. Slow re-birth restored the population to about 3,000. Reduced by another raid, it has never equalled that figure since, and the population today, including bordering hamlets, is some 1,600.

Almost within a six-hit of the cricket ground, St. Lawrence's once served as a fortress as well as a church. No wonder the spiral stairway was built so that one right-handed swordsman would have full advantage over an ascending attacker. Close to the altar the blazoned splendour of the Clifford tombs is a reminder of that astonishing woman, Anne Clifford, who asserted the rights and abilities of women centuries before the suffragettes. God-fearing, determined, capable, and infinitely kind, on the one hand she maintained the pomp of her many castles, and on the other she treated her tenants with a generous and sporting humour. A story I like particularly is of the farmer who owed her a small amount. He could afford to pay, and she held him sternly to his debt. Once it was settled, she invited him to dinner, a meal that cost more than his liability.

Of the gargoyles presiding over the main aisle, one is a scoundrel, the second on the left as you advance from the back. I would describe him as youngish, with an amused and cunning grin. I spent two summers at Appleby, and sat under him at morning service. Probably the sculptor moulded him on some contemporary spiv. The accusation may sound fantastic, but I accuse that gargoyle of theft. One weekday morning I was showing a friend of mine over St. Lawrence's. We had the church to ourselves. I paused by the spiv, to point out his human expression. In my hand was an old tweed cap, priceless with age and wear and comfort. I left this on the pew while we went up to inspect the Clifford tombs. When we came back the cap had gone and I swear that the gargoyle bore a deeper grin. I like to think that in the silent and sacred darkness of night he pulls it over his stone temples and feels a bit of a lad.

From east of Appleby the great flank of the Pennines challenges the Lake District mountains across the Eden valley. With full respect for their silence and size and their solitude, they lack the ultimately ferocious threat of some of the Lakeland fells. But they have, or at least had, their areas of danger. The Royal Armoured Corps used a range at Warcop, slinging their shells into the high nipples of Mickle Fell. There were warning notices, and only a fool like myself would have said: 'They're not firing this morning, and so I'll go aloft.' Reaching the top of Hilton Ghyll, I was encompassed by mist, started to wander, heard dull thuds, and then yelped at a crash and a flash almost on top of me. Luck sent me bolting in the right direction.

West of Appleby, and close indeed to the Lake District proper, the music of the Lyvennet reminds me of the invitation in Barrie's *Mary Rose*, except that the Lyvennet has no truck with the wistful but chuckles like a pleased and innocent child. Idling by the side of the road at Maulds Meaburn on a warm, purring June day, I glanced across at the cottages where the Lyvennet washes past their gardens under tiny bridges. Hot it was, very hot, and what happened belonged to the dreaminess of a summer day. Two boys of about ten emerged from a cottage, arm in arm. Still arm in arm, and their feet bare, they stepped into the water, and using the Lyvennet as a cool and glinting path, sauntered along through the stream and disappeared around a curve. Twenty minutes afterwards, and not far off, the Lyvennet staged another charmed episode. In a wide and shallow stretch stood a man washing a cart, while the attached horse sipped the water very much like a man enjoying a slow half-pint in a pub.

Many a garden in Windermere, Ambleside, Keswick, in fact, many a garden dotted about Cumberland, Westmorland and North Lancashire has its bordering of peculiar pieces of limestone, weird shapes that might have been designed by Picasso or borrowed from some exhibition of modern art. Most of these came from Orton Scar, a few miles out of Appleby on the road to Kendal. It would be almost reasonable to believe that this huge, white, fragmented ridge adjoining the road is inexhaustible. Among its cracks peep tiny alpines. Old trucks, loaded with pale and popular lumps, pick their bumpy and unhurried way down from the ridge. There is something about this trade that exudes restfulness and geniality. In fact, the whole high and crumpled plateau ought to be named the Land of Good Temper.

Yet it has frightening moods. Up here, above the village of Orton, I was caught in an August thunderstorm with a push bike. My cowardly reaction was to dump the bike near some whins and put a good distance between itself and me. All that shining metal looked to be a nasty neighbour under forked lightning.

Kendal, one of the doorsteps to the Lake District, houses most of the county administrative work, but still has to call small Appleby 'Sir'. Its schools teach children who come astonishing distances. Travelling in a late afternoon bus from Kendal to Appleby, the passengers mostly children, I noticed a girl of about 14 getting out beyond Orton. She made for a fell track twining up towards a remote farm. I asked the conductor about her.

'Aye,' he said, 'a gey bonnie lass. Takes her an hour and a quarter fra Kendal. Then yon trod back yum (home) is anither 25 minutes.'

She had to leave home at seven to get to school by nine. In winter both morning and evening walks along the skirt of the fell were in pitch darkness. She had the complexion of a babe and eyes that would have honoured a stained glass window.

The grey stone of Kendal wears well, and carries its history lightly. Two of its great products are linked with colour. Kendal Green was a famous cloth, known throughout the kingdom. Once upon a time this woollen material had to be sent abroad to be dyed. Enterprising Kendal merchants resented this drain on their profits. Woad was plentiful. Why not mix it with the juice of broom, so plentiful about the common lands? They were granted a charter of permission, and Kendal Green came into its own.

Kendal Brown, the snuff, is still manufactured in the town. I was offered a pinch of it at a hound-trail, sprinkled it along the back of my hand, took a sniff, and wondered whether I would lose the top of my head. The dalesman who had offered it laughed and said:

'Nay, 'twas wastin' gey good stuff on a neb (nose) like thine.'

Another product attracted sudden fame, Kendal mint-cake. When the press came out with the news that Hillary and Tensing had nibbled mint-cake on the summit of Everest, the south demanded the sweetmeat in such quantity, it vanished from the northern shops. Addicts grieved, and friends of mine said that without mint-cake their fell-walking became a greater effort.

Traffic buzzes and roars and throbs through Kendal, almost blotting out the chimes of the Town Hall clock playing the tune of John Peel. The town seethes with life. New buildings spring up, and there is a feel of growth and progress in the air. But, in truth, the town in its bowl among the widespread fells continues to look a Mecca for country folk.

Quiet weather over the Christmas holidays we reckon a double boon. The sheep above are browsing in peace; and the folk on holiday who walk or climb should come to no harm. It was on the 30th of what had been an almost docile December that a still morning changed to an ominous noon. Eb had gone up with two dogs in search of a wandering tup. The creature was well able to fend for itself, as are the yows, but because of its value we are less inclined to risk loss or damage. A ratching tup, as we call it, must be brought back to an intake or a dale meadow.

Somewhere between 11 and 12 the north-western sky changed from watery grey-blue to gun-metal. It looked as though Eb might get a soaking. Not that I worried about him landing in any trouble. He was on his native heath, familiar with every beck and gully and borran and tilt of scree. But if any visitor were out on the fell, I hoped that visitor would take warning from the sky and turn back. By all the signs, mountain rescue today would be a hopeless business.

On these rescue expeditions rock-climbers give the least trouble. No sane rock-climber climbs on his own. With two or three as a minimum, if one falls at least the other can hurry off for help and give the exact position of the casualty. Getting a victim down from a ledge on a crag-face may be tricky, but only in a minor sense. The lone walker who fails to return, or worse, the one who sets out without a word about his destination and does not arrive back, presents a problem that can be solved only by a measure of luck.

Given a partial clue, say that he was intending to ascend Scafell Pike from Langdale, we comb the popular routes. That failing, we know the places where if a walker deviated from these tracks he might come to harm, and these are searched next. If there is no result, organized searching on a large scale is put into action as soon as possible. The worst situation stems from the 'phone call made from a dale maybe ten miles away, with a message something like this : 'A man of about 30 wearing grey trousers and a fawn anorak set off from here for the fells after breakfast. He hasn't come back, and we don't know which direction he went. Can you do some-thing?' In that type of case guessing is inevitable. What astonishes me is the comparatively short time taken to find the missing person. There are exceptions. The remains of one unfortunate wanderer came to light after two years, and of another, a pilot of the R.A.F., after five months. Skating rapidly over a gruesome detail, scavenging ravens and buzzards can give a clue. Of some 30 searches in which I was involved, few took longer than six hours, and nearly all had a happy ending.

In this year of grace Mountain Rescue has an administrative efficiency, with rescue posts dotted about the Lake District, adequate equipment, stretchers, lamps, walkie-talkie sets, plentiful personnel on call. Twenty years ago, in my area, we enlisted whom we could, usually local farmers or shepherds, on the spur of the moment, and used a gate from a sheepfold as a stretcher.

Returning to Eb, he came clumping down into the stackyard while a wind moaned out of a barbaric sky, plumed and pregnant with fury. The prodigal tup he left in the pasture behind the barn, and the dogs under cover. He sat down to a plate of tatie-pot while the spasmodic moanings outside grew into continuous hissing and drum-ming, and intermittent rain spattered on the window with the hard clatter of shot. Eb was starting on rice pudding when the shot changed to a sluicing cascade so that the window glass itself seemed to be slithering and quivering.

Eb put down his spoon. 'Daft chap oop yonder.' He shook his head and told his brief story. In a shallow dip on high, a place of heather and bents with soggy mosses here and there, he had met an elderly man who asked the way to Scafell. Eb had pointed to the warning sky and said: 'Git thee back quick.' The man's answer was almost amused; he had been up here several times, and knew the Lake District fairly well; he could take care of himself. Eb's comment, blunt and to the point, had made no difference. The man was going up Scafell.

I said: 'The idiot! and he actually set off that way?'

'Aye. Daft boogger.'

There was nothing we could do then except to hope that as the weather grew worse the man grew more sensible. So often had I heard that rather proud and pardonable boast from visitors: 'Oh, I've been in the Lake District a lot, in all kinds of weather. I'm not the kind to get lost.'

By mid-afternoon the dale was a pandemonium of booming and hissing. Ash and sycamore and oak and alder shuddered in their winter nakedness, branches swaying and creaking, twigs flying through the air, water sluicing down their trunks. Only the lowest skirts of the fell opposite were visible. Racing cloud had descended to within 200 feet of the dale floor. Beneath its ragged lower fringe, emerging from the hidden fells above, gushed the whiteness of a dozen new becks. The river itself had a voice in the uproar, a deep, rumbling sound blended with a bass swishing. In the semi-darkness the froth of the new becks looked luminous.

The cows in the byre were comfortable enough, and the tups knew the most sheltered spots under the field walls. Up above the yows would be tucked beneath the screening curves of boulders. But God take care of any human being abroad on the fells. Only one course would be left open to a walker, to keep the gale behind him and plod on and on until he reached some dale, no matter how far from home. A Samson trying to walk against it would be drained and spent in half an hour.

At tea, with the light on, Derwent and I and Eb discussed the man he had met above, and Derwent said: 'Mebbe he's yum (home) be now.'

Eb took a sup from his mug. 'He'd better be. 'Tis near dark. But it 'ud hev to be yum t'other side.' He pointed eastwards. 'He'd nivver git back this way.'

The evening grew worse. I heard a creaking crash in front, and fetched a torch, and saw a great sycamore branch sprawled across a puddle. What with the winter darkness, the low cloud, and the seething rain, a car would have had no easy task to grope its way along the narrow dale road.

Around eight the telephone tinkled. It was hard to hear the speaker. No doubt some branch tapped against the line. The voice said: 'An elderly man staying with us set off for Scafell this morning and hasn't come back. Have you or any of your folk seen—?'

Eb was at hand. He dislikes the 'phone, but gave a description to the listener. Eb added: 'Reckon he'll be deid be now.'

To take out a rescue party that night would have been madness, with visibility nil and a storm of wind that nobody could walk against. After brief discussion we arranged to contact the next dale, if the 'phone there were in order, and to launch a joint search at dawn, working from east and west.

We managed to get in touch. The night outside remained a maelstrom, and late dawn offered no promise, cloud sweeping the dale floor, cold rain beating a tattoo on the windows.

'If we gaa oot,' said Eb, 'we'll see nowt. But ah'll coom if ah's wanted.'

I rang the other dale. They said it was hopeless, and absurd to risk more life to search in these conditions for someone who must already be dead. I respected their judgement. Yet there remained the gambler's instinct: I argued with myself that if by some miracle the man yet lived, there might be another miracle, that of finding him. We made up a party of six dalesmen, the three youngest and fittest to search the spine and crest of Scafell, two others to cover the medium slopes, and myself to take a roving commission in between. Ours was a sort of calculated optimism, for on setting off we could scarcely see the dale trees 50 yards away. But we had an idea that the murk was lifting. Before we parted it was agreed that we should meet, news or no news, at a certain spot at a certain time. It was the one precaution we could take as regards checking on ourselves.

Becks descending the fell had their waters blown back into the air. Dead brackens swung about and whistled, and the old heather trembled; but now and again we could see a hazy hundred yards or more; there were odd seconds free of rain; then it would come over again, sweeping towards us as aluminium rods. Where possible we moved diagonally into the wind, dodging its full power. In places where it had to be opposed, there was only one formula, a sideways ramming, knees bent, one shoulder acting as a prow; after ten side-steps, a little rest, and the head turned away to breathe out with the wind, because trying to breathe into it was a waste of effort.

Between 10.30 and 11 visibility increased to several hundred yards. The ridge of Scafell remained in flowing blindness. Where I walked on the breast below I could see fairly clearly towards the west. Untroubled sheep were nibbling with their backs to the wind, their drenched, ruffled fleeces beginning to dry out. The squelching mosses and glistening rock and sapless bents among the sparse, acid soil formed a watery picture that sometimes made it difficult for the eye to detect where the grey air ended and the grey land began. But things were improving; no doubt of that; I could see the two well below edging their way among a clutter of boulders.

Within a few minutes of the appointed time the three from above joined us. On the ridge visibility had been about 20 feet. The missing man could have been down one of the several gullies on the eastern flank of the ridge, but to search them in the masking cloud would have been like looking for a needle in a haystack; and as we all knew in our hearts by now, no human being could have survived the night up here. Snow and ice are endurable, and an experienced wanderer can make use of snow to build a shelter. But in a drenching gale heat evaporates from the wet body at a lethal rate.

We came down to the dale and passed on our negative news. The next day was raw, wild, sunless; very high black cloud sailed across a grey-green sky, but visibility was reasonable. I went up with a pair of field glasses, scanning the buttresses and gullies on the east of Scafell and the Pike. Any pale mark among those wet, dark walls of rock might lead to something. The search involved hours of scrambling up and down clutters of splintered granite, sprawls of scree, gullies where water slid whitely through shadow. A dog fox emerged from behind a boulder, looked at me, and trotted away without alarm. A buzzard circled high in the cold air, mewing.

About mid-afternoon I believed I had found the man. Some way up a steep and distant slope there was something resembling a fawn anorak, distinctly light in colour against the surrounding rock. The place was awkward to reach, beyond a run of loose fragments and uneasily perched boulders. Fifty yards from the light patch I identi-

fied it as a piece of rock broken away from a crag above, the newly
cracked surface being a shiny yellow-brown. Two hours afterwards
another pale speck high up in a gully attracted my attention. Could
that be an anorak or waterproof jacket of some kind? On the main
track below, skirting Great Moss, walked a sturdy young hiker. I
shouted at him to come up, passed him the glasses, and asked him to
use his youthful eyes. He said the object was a chunk of rock with
water trickling around it.

On the Sunday a large party of us went out in fair weather. Two of
the dalesmen who had searched the ridge on the first day headed
for a gully east of Horn Crag. They saw a woolly hat, and a few
yards lower a handkerchief showed white against scree. A little
below that lay the dead man, his head badly damaged. It seemed
plain that with the north-west gale making return impossible, he
had decided to walk with it behind him, descending the eastern
flank of the ridge for the shelter of the valley. He must have slipped
on the steep, wet rock and struck his head. We hoped he died
quickly.

I have given this account at some length because mountain rescue
is as much a feature of the Lake District as clipping sheep or felling
trees. Of the annual visitors, at least a half of them, I imagine, walk
the fells; and of those who come to grief, the majority are young;
youth, rightly, likes to be daring, likes to take risks. Another aspect,
less obvious, is the personal philosophy of the walker. A hosteller
starts off in all the vigour of young manhood. Something goes wrong,
a change in the weather, a mistake in direction. There is a swing
of the pendulum from gay buoyancy to scared depression. Loss of
heart reduces the circulation, and the flesh grows cold. The veteran
in years has lived long enough to take a different attitude. By this
time tomorrow, he tells himself, he will be laughing at today's
episode. That sort of outlook, and a sensible outlook it is, can serve
as a guardian angel to a lost walker.

CHAPTER ELEVEN

January

In the dark days of January many a dalesman would like to cut a thick slice off the top of the opposite fell and let in any rising sun that may be gladdening the higher world. Even farms facing south can be deprived of an hour at both the beginning and end of the day. Where I live the sun reaches us about 9.15 in the first week of the year, glides through flat orbit just above the lip of the fell, and vanishes at 3 p.m. This is Greenwich Mean Time. We hold no brief for Daylight Saving in winter. Nights are so black, it is wise to keep the eyes closed for some seconds when emerging from the house, to adjust the sight. Walking down a dale involves more baffling darkness than walking up it, for the higher fells, even in the dense loom of night, stand out as dim ebony shapes.

Often the early part of January is mild, quiet, harmless. A visitor might compare it favourably with the climate of the south. Then one day the air grows dry and utterly still. There is a smell of frost, and the stone walls glisten; the clear night sky presages a cold spell free of snow. While this lasts nobody will be complaining, but when leaden cloud swells up in the east, and muffled moaning creeps into the quietude, we know that the worst is on its way.

Folk living in the western dales, Dunnerdale, Eskdale, Wasdale and Ennerdale, insist that their winters are less savage than the more inland places. The Gulf Stream is their reasonably near neighbour. It certainly makes a difference. In the blanched and shuddering winter-spring of 1947 the only reliable mode of travel was by the coastal railway. Here and there, between its embankment and the beach, are strips of grazing. Sitting in a compartment and heading north it was extraordinary to glance right, then left. Eastward all was white, building up to the final barricade of the tallest fells, great white curves rearing into the cold air as if they were frozen to their very hearts. Westward, between the embankment and the shore, cattle browsed among greenery, stressing, in sunny phases, the lilac-blue of the Solway. Hoggs, lambs born the previous spring, were enjoying the privilege of wintering along the coast, nibbling the sea-washed Cumberland turf while their mothers aloft were burying their muzzles in the hard snow to thaw admission to the starved herbage beneath.

I had business that day at Egremont, some distance from the nearest station. The wide main street had been cleared of snow, and the town generally was unaffected by the weather. Perhaps the Normans considered this geniality when they built the castle and made the place the seat of military government for north-west England. They would have found a yet milder site had they gone up to Silloth. In a book published about 1830 I read: 'Silloth, on the Cumberland side of the Solway, is a pleasant, peaceful resort, much esteemed by those ladies and gentlemen who seek convalescence among warm and equable airs.'

A casual glance at Egremont would scarcely evoke thoughts of the romantic. A second look, directly at the ruins of the castle, brings a change of mind. Studying the ancient, robust design, it is easy to accept that from here were proclaimed edicts affecting a big area of the North. Egremont's history includes a fair share of excitement and blue-blooded splendour. There was the chilling and yet splendid tale of the Horn of Egremont, which hung at the main gate; none but the lord of the castle could sound it. At the time of the Crusades the lord was Sir Eustace de Lucy, and the heir his brother, Hubert.

Moved by the appeals of Christendom, the two decided to go out to Palestine; before they left, Sir Eustace solemnly discussed the future with his brother.

'If I fall in Palestine,' he said, 'do you return, and blow the horn, and take possession?'

During the campaign, temptation to own the castle drove Hubert to planning murder. He hired brigands to drown his brother in the

river Jordan. The way clear, he came back to England, and unable to blow the horn, entered the castle by night and took possession. Conscience troubled him. To blunt his remorse he maintained a programme of wine, women and song.

Still hanging by the main gate was the horn, described by Wordsworth centuries later in the lines

> *which none could sound,*
> *No one upon living ground,*
> *Save he who came as rightful heir,*
> *To Egremont's domain and castle fair.*

On an evening of revelry, despite all the noise, the usurper heard the note of the horn, and knew that his end was nigh. Somehow his brother must have escaped the brigands.

Hubert fled; Sir Eustace took back the castle. In the following months Hubert begged and was granted forgiveness, and entered a monastery.

It was Wordsworth again who wrote the poem about the Boy of Egremont, the unlucky youngster who, had he lived, might have changed the history of England and Scotland. Alice Romilly, of Egremont castle, fourth lady of Allerdale, married William Fitz-Duncan. They had a son named William, and by reason of his male and female ancestors seemed likely to succeed to both the English and Scottish crowns. At the age of 15 he went to stay with some relatives living near Bolton Abbey, close to the notorious stretch of the river Wharfe known as the Strid. One day, out hunting, he came to the edge of the Strid, not much more than four feet wide. To an athletic lad it seemed nothing of a jump. The leash of his greyhound tied to his girdle, he took a leap, and the hound jerked back. They were drowned in that wicked narrowness of water where the eroded banks are concave to a great depth and a victim is trapped like a fly in a bottle. The forester who had been with him brought the heart-breaking news to his mother, adding: 'What is good for a bootless Bene? (What remains when prayer is useless?)'

She answered: 'Bootless bayl brings endless sorrow.'

To this day the Strid has an ugly name, and rumour claims that anybody falling in has little chance.

Because of its importance as a centre of northern government, Egremont had a considerable code of laws and statutes. Within the limits of the town it was illegal to lop the paw of a dog; outside this area, to prevent a dog from chasing the royal game, and yet enabling it to act as a watchdog, the lopping of one paw was compulsory. Another rule, of a kind that must have made Satan grin, imposed a penalty on any burgess for seducing a woman. He had to pay a fine of three shillings to his lord. Perhaps the grand folk at the castle kept hoping that the burgesses would play fast and loose.

An almost quaint item of more recent interest concerns the dual use of the name of Egremont in titles. On the Tory side is the Earl of Egremont, formerly secretary to Mr. Macmillan. On the Labour side is Baroness Gaitskell of Egremont, widow of Hugh Gaitskell. Dotted about this area are several houses and wide acres that belonged to the Gaitskells, including Yeorton Hall, a few miles away. The house still stands: the long approach to it, heralded by an avenue of trees, has grown into a green carpet. The family produced in Hugh a typical Cumbrian who had the courage of his convictions. As the years pass by more and more folk believe that had he lived it would have been better for England.

When the politicians were discussing how to save money by cutting down the railway system, one of their targets of economy became the line between Barrow and Whitehaven. They argued, rightly, that it served a small population. Someone whispered apologetically that in several areas there was no bus service, no public transport whatever; it might be difficult for local folk without private cars. Promptly a well-meaning minister promised to meet the need with a direct coastal road service. There came another apologetic whisper; because of the estuaries there could be no direct service, unless they turned the track into a road, for the only bridges were those along the railway. As for the alternative, roads across the fells, these were blocked by snowdrifts in winter. It was a blow to the minister's gay project. A diesel still serves the district.

Snow in Lakeland can multiply the mileage of a journey by three, or four, or five. We all rely so much upon the passes, if they become blocked we have to get out a map and scan it carefully. Hardknot, Wrynose, Birker Moor, Whicham Valley, Whinlatter, Newlands, Dunmail Raise, the list of white barricades mounts up and up, as does the alternative mileage. On a January Sunday five young fell-walkers descended into our valley by mistake: they had lost direction in snow-clouds wavering about the tops. As the foot can walk, they were eleven miles from where they wanted to be; but they were tired, and asked if it might be possible to hire a car. I 'phoned a garage proprietor. Had it been summer, he would have driven them over that same 11 miles. Now ice and drifts were a complete bar to wheels. He worked out the nearest negotiable route for a car. The journey there and back totalled just over 100 miles.

County roadmen are ready to deal with these hazards. They seem to react at once to conditions, without waiting for orders from above. Their snow-ploughs are in position at points of vantage. They cleave along, cutting a wide furrow: those with hot air and a brush make the best job of it. Ploughing alone, without any scattering of grit, sometimes leads to the last state being worse than the first. On a Sunday of thick snow I had floundered along a field path to an afternoon service at church. It was over my knees, a weary affair of lifting each leg high, plunging deep, snow sucking at the ankles and calves. After the service I made for the dale road. A snow-plough had been along about three o'clock, in sunshine. It left a half-inch of smooth, softish snow that hardened to a skating rink as the sun dropped behind the fells between half-past three and four. At every little rise of the road I found myself sliding backwards. Progress on all fours was little better. A car would have been helpless. The answer, I found, was to edge along under the snowy road banks, my finger-tips clawing in between the boulders of the flanking wall. So might a drunken crab pick its way home.

The most efficient, fairy-godmother performance of roadmen I ever met was on the long steepness of Grizebeck Hill rising up to Gawthwaite Moor, the main road leading on to Greenodd and Newby Bridge. Shortly after the dawn of an utterly fickle day, snow, thaw, rain, snow, thaw, a friend and I were driving from Broughton in Furness to Grizebeck Village. Dampness spattered beneath the tyres. We drove on contentedly, assured that we were finished with bother.

As we ascended the lower reaches of Grizebeck Hill the road surface froze suddenly. The speed of that freeze-up savoured of black magic. Our wheels scuffled, failed, and we started to slide backwards. My friend juggled with the wheel, and neatly brought us to a diagonal halt, the back wheels against the bank.

'And here,' he said, 'we remain.'

Within minutes we heard a chugging below. A county truck came up backwards, spraying its grit in front of itself. It gritted the whole hill, returned, sprayed extra grit about our wheels, gave us a shove, and we were up and away.

So much for snow on the roads. A deep white blanket over the fells will bring a tinge of anxiety even to the most philosophic fell-farmer. Nobody worries about a few days of it. After a week, with a hard frost ruling, some of the sheep may be in trouble. Many find their way down to the dale, snatching at leafless branches, or standing high on hind legs and nibbling at bark. They jump the walls of the few farm gardens and ravage the evergreens. All of these can take care of themselves. The sheep in danger are those that have found shelter up above, avoiding a blizzard by staying below a tall rock-face or under the sizeable bank of a beck.

It was these that Derwent and Eb and I sought in the third week of an Arctic January spell. We collected two dogs, Gyp and Spy, after breakfast and started up from the stackyard, Eb and I with spades and Derwent carrying a long, thin pole. It had been a night of east wind bringing across hard, granulated flakes like buckshot that formed a crust on the walls. Now the wind had lessened a little, and a chill blueness reigned in the sky, though smoky fingers clawing forward from the east promised more blizzards soon. In the tilted rake the snow was two feet deep. Derwent preferred gumboots. Eb and I wore shepherds' boots softened with warm castor oil. There is division of opinion about this treatment. Some condemn it, and recommend bacon fat. Some swear by a skin of good boot polish.

Our feet sank into variable depths. The dogs flurried and scurried with their own technique, a forward lunge, an apparent subsiding into the softness, and then a twisting wrench of the belly that took them forward and upward. Icicles adorned the granite walls, and over the boulders in the lower courses were tight white splodges as if children had thrown blobs of blancmange mixed with cement. Beyond the gate, although we knew the ground intimately, it was hard to be sure of every step. Suddenly I was in snow half-way up to my right thigh. From there to my ankle tingled a dank coldness. From my ankle to the sole of my foot it felt wet and warm. I had forgotten the curve of a beck crossing just above the top of the rake. It rises from a spring a thousand feet up, retaining its warmth, and the blizzard had hidden it from sight under a continuous bridge of snow.

The trod, the drift-road used for the passage of sheep, was difficult to discern; flanking dead brackens and heather had been submerged by the snow, and the whole breast was a smoothness broken only by the largest boulders and the dark, jagged ribbon of the main beck, its surface iced, a trickle of water beneath; it resembled a huge and shaggy thermometer. Fox-footings marked the snow ahead. Like the rest, Reynard would be hungry. But he has the patience of his species, a patience that will hold him dead still among the leaves of a winter rhododendron until an unlucky thrush or blackbird perches within leap.

Eb sniffed. 'Fair nips thy neb.'

Derwent laughed. 'Mebbe some lass 'll knit a muff fur it.'

Within minutes his neb was warm. We were still 300 feet below the first terrace of the fell, plodding up gradients from 30° to 40°. What with that and the clutching of the snow, keeping moving generated a welcome warmth. We crossed the beck again, this time by a culvert of boulders hidden beneath white plumpness. Beyond it a yow was standing in a queer attitude.

'Look yon,' said Eb.

He pointed at the trouble. From the top of her poll to the hump of her withers stretched a board of ice. In the night she must have been facing the blizzard head to wind, a not uncommon mishap. Gripped like this it was hard for her to make any attempt to sniff about in the snow and nibble at fragments of browsing. The dogs preventing her from scuttling off, Eb broke the board with the handle of his knife. She whickered, walked away, stuck her muzzle over the rim of the inhospitable beck and found a few odd bents.

When we came in sight of the first tarn, Derwent let out his favourite expression: 'By—!' That and 'Gocks!' are his two innocent expletives. He was smiling with admiration at the troubled surface. It had frozen during a fierce gale, and was a hotch-potch of paralysed waves, the angles of them giving different tintings and etchings to the ice. I wondered what sort of orchestra it would provide prior to the thaw. No wonder the ancients believed that devils were about when the ice of these tarns and lakes groaned and screeched in the agony of stress and strain. Eb talked of a hard winter in his boyhood and how the water of a small tarn gradually subsided beneath the rigid lip of ice. A lad went sliding there, fell through, and instead of being drowned, splashed into a foot of water.

We began to edge slowly towards the north-east where the snow beneath a crag-face showed a kind of shadow that had no right to be there. The dogs scampered and scurried ahead, sniffed, started a concerned yelping. We knew by now what the shadow was, grease from sheep below beginning to stain the purity above. Very carefully Derwent tested with his pole. We began to dig, and the dogs assisted as if they were scooping for rabbits.

Fifteen yows were in that drift, and none had come to any great harm. But they deserved a convalescent treatment of cake and hay. After all, in 14 weeks they had to present new life to the world. With Gyp as assistant, Eb took them off down to the dale. Derwent, Spy and I moved across slowly to a wide, shallow basin threaded by another beck. In the distance, blanched fells stabbed sharp against the skyline, immaculate in their whiteness, deathly in their sterile beauty. We were lucky. Our grazing stints face south and climb to no more than 1,500 feet. Now they offered little except heather and cotton-grass; poorish feeding, hidden by snow, but accessible to the nuzzling of a hungry yow. Those tall hills yonder would mean starvation if this hard spell went on another two or three weeks. I thought of the 1947 disaster. Some flockmasters lost 80% of their sheep. Of those that survived, many more died because winter changed abruptly to summer, the thaw sounding like the music of many flutes as the water flowed beneath the sun and the grasses leapt up to greet the warmth. After austerity here was a glut, and sheep died from over-eating.

In the bowl we disturbed a couple of dozen yows sprawled on a ledge along the rocky rim of the beck. These we drove towards a barren breast of the higher fells. They blared resentfully, and no doubt would return to their haven tonight or tomorrow. In the meanwhile, up there where the wind was a sweeping besom, the snow lay sparse and they would find easy grazing.

'Aye,' said Derwent, ''tis hard. But thou has to be cruel to be kind. Ee—Spy! Git awa!'

Snow is supposed to be beautiful, particularly where no dirt can sully its purity. But as I looked around at whiteness, whiteness, smothering tilts and hollows, bents and scree, mosses and boulders, tall fells and low hummocks, a blanched world saved from final immaculacy by the jagged black scratches of gullies and becks, I longed for spring.

We started to return through a series of hollows screened by ridges. Turning a curve we came upon a group of three foxes sprawled in the snow and enjoying the thin warmth of the sun. Spy gave tongue. They arose in no hurry and lolloped over a shoulder of fell. Spy returned, tongue out and panting hard.

'Them's gaan to be a nuisance, happen cold nip hauds.'

I nodded. Hunting in these conditions was a waste of time. Scent would be too high, or non-existent. Plain, hard frost without snow was an equal handicap. Reynard would enjoy an easy season. As for shortage of food, he has the advantage of an indiscriminate palate. Sheep alive or dead, rabbits, birds, beetles, he enjoys the lot.

Tramping, sliding, edging down to the dale, the only two humans among miles of crumpled country, we talked about town life. Derwent reckoned that a day or two of it was gey fine. After that—.

He shook his head. Nay. A chap looked up from street to sky, and glanced at cloud, and it meant nowt. If he looked up from dale, or edge of village, he could tell if it was 1,500 or 2,000.

He said firmly : 'In a town there's nowt to guide a chap.'

Snow and ice are certainly Reynard's friends. A long and bitter spell will paralyse hunting and create a dark cloud of dread over the lambing season. Of lowland hunting I have had no experience, and can offer no opinion. But this is a grim certainty, that unless foxes were kept in reasonable check among the Lake District, then sheep-farming would come to an end. Kindly folk without knowledge of the subject grow angry over blood sports. They have my sympathy. At first thought, to hunt a creature seems to be heartless, unforgiveably cruel. Yet nobody objects to the necessary measures taken to keep down mice and rats.

I once took part in a television debate on hunting. The two who spoke against it were a very likeable parson and a youngish M.P. who became a Cabinet Minister. This latter said: 'If foxes are such a nuisance, why don't you put down poison?' I explained that it would kill our dogs and our sheep. Then why not traps? The answer was: 'And trap our dogs and sheep?' He tried another tack. We should shoot the foxes. He was taken aback to learn that on our hunts some of the farmers bring out a gun and have a pot at the fox. It was pointed out to him that without hounds to put him up, Reynard would stay snug in some rocky ghyll or clutter of boulders or patch of heather. A score of men might pass within 20 yards and not see him; but he would see them. Even if they disturbed him, he would lollop a short distance and go to ground again in one of the myriad holes.

'Well,' said the M.P., 'couldn't you fill up the holes?'

This was an honest question, not facetious. It proved beyond all peradventure that the nature of Lakeland is still a closed book to a surprising number of the public.

The likeable parson admitted that he had never witnessed a hunt.

He said: 'It isn't necessary. I don't have to see thugs attacking an old lady to know that it's abominable. Neither do I have to see hounds chasing a fox and killing it.'

I almost hated to point out that his comparison was ludicrous. The fox is the bandit. The lambs and yows—and poultry—are the old lady. And if the iron hand of winter stiffens the land for long, foxes stay wick, the local term for plentiful, and farming suffers grievously.

Eventually, the parson said:

'That's all very well. But the odds are so unfair. A couple of dozen hounds and a lot of men against one small fox.'

I suppose he was thinking in terms of a stylish hunt, satiny horses, scarlet coats and elegant hats, a gay cavalcade of pomp and circumstance careering over fields, jumping low hedges, cantering along the skirts of gentle spinneys. He had to be told that horses in our part of the world would break their necks in the first minute or two; that if Reynard swung away up the fells, we humans might see no more for the rest of the hunt; that every so often Reynard led hounds to their death by racing to a sheer edge with them in close pursuit, then digging in his sharp claws and swinging around while the hounds, their pads unsuited to a sudden check, pitched over into eternity.

Suppose that iron-hard January has softened to a thaw towards the end of the month. Word goes round that the hunt will be meeting next morning at the small grey farm squatting beneath the steep breast on the other side of the dale. Eb and Derwent and I set off for the spot a bit before eight. Despite the thaw, we blow into our hands. The air strikes raw under a west-north-west wind, and the patches of ragged cloud unleash spatters of chilly rain. Eb wears jacket and trousers colourless with age, a shirt with a stud and no collar, and clogs. Derwent has pulled on an old oilskin. His feet are tucked into gumboots. As we approach the hump-back bridge over the river we can see the barn of the small grey farm. Hounds have been spending the night there. The tall young huntsman crosses the stackyard, opens the door, and out they spill, white and tan, lemon and white, tan and black, jostling around him. By the farmhouse some dozen shepherds and farmers and boys are gathered, stamping their feet and slapping their arms to keep warm.

Somebody calls: 'Hoo's fettle, Eb?'

Eb grins. 'A sup o' rum 'ud gaa doon well.'

Up the rough gravel trod from below creaks a push-bike, the Master pedalling slowly and leading a pair of Border terriers. They will be needed if a fox heads for some borran of boulders and 'binks' inside them. The short and yellowish winter grasses vibrate under a blast from the distant Solway. Down a dark ghyll wounding the fell-breast a thread of water is being sprayed by the wind. The dead, rusty brackens creak and shiver; the greenery of mosses in the damp spots somehow has a sullen effect: naked rock varies, black, shadowed indigo, dull silver. Just above the lip of the fell a buzzard slides out, mewing, stalls for seconds, and floats away on the wings of the wind.

The huntsman sounds a note on his small horn. Hounds are pattering behind him as he heads up a trod between a thick scattering of savins, juniper bushes where eight months earlier the red-backed shrikes were nesting, impaling their victims, bluebottles, flies, and such, on the thorns to form a handy larder.

The huntsman keeps going with his long, unchanging stride, knees bent, toes turned out a little. As we follow on, hounds patter across to a tangle of old heather and begin to mill around, giving tongue. A young shepherd lets out a sudden yell, a shrill ululation, swings up his pointing hand. There it is, a rufous flicker flowing over a tilt of scree. The music of the hounds echoes back from the rock.

Eb jerks his thumb at a col cutting through the terrace of the fell. 'He'll gaa yon.'

And yon he goes, a big dog-fox up a gradient of one in two, effortless, under the protrusion of a buttress, over a platform of sparse soil and bents, between a sprinkling of boulders, into the shadowed chill of a gully and straight up the other side. By the rate he moves, he has an empty stomach. No fox that had fed well within the last hour or two could travel at that speed. Hounds are becoming pale blobs well below him. As for ourselves, we can do nothing but stand and watch, excitement helping us to forget our cold noses. If fox and hounds top the ridge and keep on east or south, we may see nothing more of today's hunt. Human legs are soon tamed to a walk, and lungs to a protesting gasp, when folk try to follow the four-legged in this country.

Eb nods thoughtfully. 'He'll break back. Aye.'

A few of the younger men doubt it. The others accept Eb's prophecy. According to the old brigade, he has the gift of a former

Master, of knowing what the fox is going to do before it knows itself.

Fox and pale blobs have vanished over the skyline. We grow more conscious of the damp rawness. Across the dale the higher peaks are being wrapped in slate-coloured scarves.

Derwent yells: 'By—!' His voice and gesture are full of admiration. There it is, high up and away to our right, descending at a diagonal, a reddish bobbing making for a borran below. Reynard has a lead of at least 50 yards beyond the leading hound. We turn and run, the older ones jog-trotting, the younger scampering, hopping over boulders, laughing with the thrill of the moment. In a matter of seconds the fox has binked, gone to earth, or in this case, gone to rock, deep inside a pile of boulders. Round and round the hounds are milling and giving mournful tongue.

Here the two small Border terriers come into their own. The Master slips them into a crevice and they disappear eagerly. Eb moves with cautious steps. These borrans are tricky spots, sometimes trigger-balanced. The clinking of odd boulders as hounds move over them proves their looseness.

There is another chilly wait, the huntsman crouching and listening for any sound. No snarling or noises of battle come up through the chinks.

Derwent says anxiously: 'Mebbe them's jumped doon and can't git back.'

That is always the risk attending terriers in a borran. They may leap down a rock-face of six or seven feet, to find no further progress that way; the only return is by an upward spring, and since they can leap down further than they can leap up, they may be trapped. Then the followers forget the fox, and spend the day, and perhaps another day, removing tons of boulders, some demanding infinite caution, before they can release the entombed terriers.

The minutes tick on, until from the bowels of the borran rises a snarling. Despite the alerted hounds, the fox is out and clear. There must be a series of underground chinks like a tunnel, for a red flash is topping a knoll 50 yards away. The bristling terriers emerge at our feet. Hounds are streaking for the knoll. We all start running, and some of the youngsters are yelling as well, to Eb's disapproval. As a purist he feels that such behaviour is out of keeping.

Reynard is swerving up again, under the shoulder of a very steep buttress marked by narrow ledges that end nowhere. Eb comes to a halt, and his voice rises prophetic.

'He'll bet (beat) 'em. He'll coom doon them ledges, and they'll be cragfast. Watch yonder!'

The fox emerges, rippling out of the head of the gully and pauses at the top of the buttress. There is something inviting about that pause, as if daring the hounds to follow up and over. Seconds later he drops lightly to the ledge beneath, from that to the next, lands on a slender shelf of rock that thins away into nothingness at each end. At least 30 feet below lies a hog-back of thin soil and scree with a small centre of yellow-grey nardus grass. Maybe one or two of the young boys with us believe he is trapped. They are soon to learn otherwise.

Hounds are streaming up under the shoulder and out upon the summit. In vain the huntsman's horn tries to stop them.

'Bide!' we yell imploringly, 'bide!'

Two or three hesitate, but the rest are leaping down, and with a flick of the pads on the topmost ledge, jump on down to the second. Some of them pause. Half a dozen, without hesitating, poise to launch themselves below. At the same time the fox springs outwards, coils, falls like a furry ball and lands in the nardus patch. From there it strolls, quite slowly across a fan of scree, and some of us almost expect it to stick a paw to its muzzle in rude triumph.

There are six hounds on that lowest shelf, with no room for another. One or two of their mates above are jerking their heads and shoulders to and fro, as if gauging the best way to join them. The huntsman is using his voice instead of the horn, his shouts echoing back from the buttress. The Master points to the grey farm far below.

'Git doon quick, some o' you. There's ropes in yon van.'

Three of the younger ones set off, making for a stripe of smallish loose stones where they can gain time by scree-running, boots striding and slithering as the stuff slides with them, shoulders and head well back, since a forward fall might mean a sadly grazed face or elbows scratched and bruised. The half dozen hounds on the shelf are jostling a little, but the reassuring voice of the huntsman keeps them steady.

We blow on our hands and flap them against our shoulders while waiting for the ropes. A Lancashire farmer from just over the border describes the fox as 'a reet coonning boogger'. Eb laughs, and calls it 'a gey smart 'un'. We all agree that it deserves its freedom and wish it luck.

The three young chaps come hurrying up with the ropes, ascending bracken slopes and rock and scree with the rolling ease of those who often earn a bit extra by laying the scent for the hound-trails. The young huntsman, roped, persuades the hounds on the two upper ledges to stand on their hind legs and be bunked up and over. Next, very carefully, he is lowered half-way to the shelf below, where he gets hold of a hound behind its front legs, thumbs against the chest, and thrusts it up to the ledge above. The rest, invited to stretch up on their hind legs, are coaxed similarly to safety.

This episode of the winning fox is far from unique. A few years ago the Eskdale and Ennerdale hounds had put up a fox in a spinney near the foot of Birker Force. For a while it discarded scent by paddling through the Esk. We lost touch, the hounds searching and edging in a rather aimless way further down the valley. We were close to Dalegarth Hall, the old granite house with rounded stone chimneys, home of the Austhwaites before the conquest, and of the ancient family of Stanley since medieval times. Waiting for something to happen, I glanced in the direction of Underbank, a farmhouse on Stanley land so hidden below the skirt of the fell, a man might pass daily within a 100 yards of the place, and never dream of its existence. It seemed to me that the fox we sought was as clever at hiding as the house.

Not that Underbank had been entirely successful in its secrecy. During the Civil War a Royalist on the run sought refuge with the Stanley of that period. He hid the man in Underbank. Either Cromwellian troops were extra clever searchers, or an informer lurked in the dale. The Royalist was ferreted out, and Stanley mulcted by a heavy fine. Years later he received a double pardon, one signed by Cromwell and the other by Fairfax. The two documents, flanked by the portrait of the pardoned Stanley, are over the dining-room fireplace.

Waiting under an oak, and recalling the story, I half-wished that the fox we were after might get clean away. The wish crumbled under an abrupt burst of music from hounds. It came from a rough spinney adjoining Stanley Ghyll beck. As we hurried through the gateway in the wall we could hear the brushing of pads across dead leaves and pine needles. The stony trod ascending the ghyll, first one side, then the other, reaches a steepness unfit for many an in-experienced human. There have been landslides. Twice unlucky walkers have fallen over the edge and lost their lives.

As Eb and I made for the trod, he said: 'Bet yon fox is oop til (to) nay good.'

Although midwinter, the screens of rhododendron leaves masked our view ahead, and what with these, and the tree trunks and the curving banks of the beck, we could judge only by sound and not by sight. We reckoned that fox and hounds were somewhere about the third footbridge, a place where even a fool would take care. Edging along the trod, well above the ghyll and beyond the second bridge, we caught sight of the huntsman crossing the third. Beyond this is the force or waterfall itself, the airy trod to the east, and a sheer grey cliff to the west.

Nobody knew exactly what happened in the next minute. Putting together the evidence of sounds and a few scanty optical clues, we reckoned that the fox had slowed down deliberately and made for the edge, two hounds close behind. At the last moment, sharp claws acting as a brake, it swivelled about, back among the undergrowth. The hounds, their pads wet, shot straight over and plunged to death.

In the Lake District proper there are five fell packs, the Eskdale and Ennerdale, Coniston, Mellbreak, Blencathra, and Ullswater. Be-tween them they cover such extents of country as to seem beyond possibility to a lowland hunt. The apparently impossible is achieved by the huntsman and his hounds staying in different areas for several days at a stretch, the huntsman as the guest of some farmer, and the hounds in the farmer's barn. Boulders, dizzy heights, scree, tall jungles of old heather, dank, shuddering gullies, swift becks, woodland, swamps, the very sea-shore, all come alike to the hounds. The pack may be lost for half a day, and individual hounds for days together. Somebody 'phones the news that the pack is in a far-off dale, and the huntsman sets off in a van to collect them. Stray hounds at the end of a run will call at a farm for board and lodging, in no hurry to rejoin the rest. Next morning they resume their casual saunter towards home. They may look thin, despite a diet of flesh and porridge. Most of them, boarded out in the off-season of summer, grow plump on minor exercise.

Repeating a solemn fact, without hunting there could be no fell-farming. Three foxes in every four escape. It is a business, not an elegant social event. Well-meaning abolitionists hint that followers have no right to enjoy it. This implies that they have no right to get excited. And here the argument becomes reduced *ad absurdum*.

CHAPTER TWELVE

February

A village barber who used to cut my hair for tuppence when I was a boy insisted that the old saying 'February fill-dyke' held little truth, because the original spelling had been 'full-dyke'; the fullness lingered from January rains, and February itself shed few tears. Perhaps he was right, though the saying must have been born in the south, for to us of the Lake District, a dyke is a wall. I have seen every kind of February, the dry, the wet, the frozen, the mild, and sometimes think that the best of these is the frozen, providing that snow withholds its white pall. To anybody who knows our widespread mosses, leg-sapping stretches of sphagnum, seeves, bog-myrtle and general squelch, a dry crisp walk across the lot has a flavour of triumph.

There are worse jobs than spreading muck on a chill but stilly February afternoon. A man with the skill could work and think of something else at the same time, spreading a pile a minute with a swing of his arms and a jerk of his elbows, the quiet, dun fells watching him benevolently and a few chaffinches sprinkling along the fringes to pick up odd seeds. It may be that the ancient adage 'where there's muck there's money' originated in the fields. The townsman has no time to realize that our best farming stems from muck, not chemicals. But if he has a garden of his own and a pride in it he will certainly pay well for a bucket of horse-dung.

Because the Lakeland fields are so often small, and their gateways narrow, difficult entrances for machinery, mechanization came late. I was scaling muck by hand when lowland farms regarded such methods as primitive. Now everybody uses the mechanized spreader.

February

Before we changed over to it a strange thing happened on a dull, dry February day. The cow-muck I was scaling had been brought from the byre to the midden and from the midden to the field. In the middle of scaling a forkful I noticed a glint among the fragmented stuff. I crossed to where it had fallen, and picked up a pearl. It was so absurd, I could only make one guess, that the children had been playing with a toy necklace and broken it somewhere near the midden. Before knocking off, five more pearls were revealed as the fork scattered its load. A woman neighbour happened to call, and in a joking way I said we were growing pearls. She looked at one, and her eyes went wide. The previous autumn she had lost a good pearl necklace in a haymow, and we had bought some hay from her. We hunted up and down the field and eventually extracted from the odorous muck every pearl bar one, and the bent silver clasp. The parable about not casting pearls before swine ought to have included cows.

Excepting the hardy few prepared to challenge any kind of weather, visitors in February are unknown. They flock here in the late spring, charmed by the peeping pastel shades; they know the full green of our bracken-cloaked world in the summer, and the bronze and orange of autumn; but the dog days they leave alone to the locals. They may be wise, since the gulf between their way of living and ours is great. Mrs. Town-Smith shops in the morning, not very conscious of the weather, meets her friends for coffee in some smart tea-shop, perhaps plays bridge in the afternoon. During the course of the day, she may have passed thousands of strangers. Mrs. Dale-Todd does her house-work in the morning, feeds the hens, notices that the cloud is down to 1,500 feet, watches a buzzard stalling over the fell opposite, gets the men's dinner ready by 12, walks down to the hamlet in the afternoon to call on a crony. During the course of the day she has passed no stranger. She has seen a total of nine folk, every one of them well-known to her.

Mrs. Town-Smith will have been in sight and sound of hundreds of cars. Mrs. Dale-Todd will have seen the school-car, which came up to collect the youngsters from the farm at the head of the dale, a tractor, a cattle-wagon, and maybe two other cars unknown to her

31 *Dry stone walling in Cumberland*

and therefore arousing her curiosity. Should anybody from a town say: 'But how on earth can you tolerate such loneliness in the winter?' she will smile and point out that she would find it more lonely in a town. Winter life in a Lakeland dale has more intimacy than that of summer. The tiny things, lichens on the walls, a robin singing in a bare larch, a wisp of cloud like a scarf wrapped about the head of the fell, a tup (ram) rubbing itself against the roughness of a boulder, these are more personal than any crowded street, or road clogged up with a snarl of traffic. As for the evening hours—and sometimes the afternoon—she has the Women's Institute, a feminine democracy unequalled by anything else. Apart from the lecturers, they provide their own entertainment, and everything runs smoothly on a shoestring.

Only illness or impossibly deep snow will keep her away from a W.I. meeting. These days most of them have cars available. But on a black, soaking night I have met a farmer's wife crossing a desolate moor to meet her W.I. friends. The darkness, the hidden miles of dead heather and rocks and bleak emptiness held no fears. A strange sound and a paleness looming up out of the night would have found her unalarmed, she being used to stray sheep.

Mrs. Dale-Todd knows how to cook, how to help on the farm, and how to laugh. At a Group Meeting where I lectured the chief feature of the evening was a sketch called 'The W.I. through the Ages'. The daughter of the previous vicar started the ball rolling. She came on dressed as a Stone Age member, wearing long string as hair, a hearth-rug around her middle, and carrying a stone club. The rest of the exhibits were in similar vein, and I doubt if many professional programmes could have rivalled it.

Of all the February weathers, probably mist deserves most homage. On Lakeland roads it never brews a density that should be dangerous to any but the stupid. On the fells it plays tricks worthy of Puck. Its thickening and thinning and drifting and changing of direction under airs that apparently have no cause, its power to magnify preposterously, these are the mysteries of a magician. Few without experience of fell mist can imagine its variety of performance. In modest lowland country it will cheat the veteran. I recall a farmer who went out of his house, across the stackyard, entered his largest field and lost himself for half an hour. On the open fell, among hummocks, ridges, scree slopes, tangles of heather, secretive becks that never seem to descend, the wanderer without a compass can blunder in circles or reach the brink of sudden death.

It was a blind February day that I ascended the fell opposite about four in the afternoon. I was walking simply for exercise, zig-zagging up a peat-trod built centuries ago to supply the nearest farm in the dale. As I went up, the damp rock kept unwinding itself out of the mist, clearly, unmistakeably. At the top I followed the trod westward, along the lip of the fell. There were tiny, almost indeterminate sounds, the faint flutter of a bird, moisture dripping from a stunted rowan, the dull scrape of a yow among the heather. Since I knew the route as well as the back of my own hand, I kept on: I had no intention of diverting from it.

Minutes later I heard voices in the mist. They came from an invisible moss to the west of the trod, a squelchiness threaded by a small beck. They were the voices of several young men, and I guessed them at once to be Youth Hostellers who had come from the further dale, some miles southward, lost their track, and were following the curves of the beck.

I must have started thinking of something else. Their voices began to recede, and were almost out of hearing when sudden warning lit up my mind. They were following a beck that ended in a sheer drop, an overhang and a buttress below that were nothing but emptiness for a hundred feet. Unless they knew exactly what they were doing—.

I turned and ran, shouted and shouted, veered from the trod among wet dead brackens and patches of slurry and soggy mosses. Luck tore a split in the mist. There they were, four of them, their leader within a few strides of the edge. My desperate shouting brought them across to me.

Within a week Derwent and I were lost in mist among unknown surroundings that seemed worse than any fell. At the beginning of the previous November 200 of our hoggs had been sent down to winter on the saltings of an estuary. We chose a peaceful, semi-sunny day to visit them, Derwent and Eb and I driving down an hour after midday, Eb smoking his pipe in the back. The sky was stilly, lemon and grey, and the high fells behind us had a faint softness about them, as though clad in moleskin. Presently we left the flanking stone walls behind, turned along a rough lonnin between naked hedges. Ahead lay the estuary, a dull glimmer of wet sand and mud, with shallow, silvery drainage channels and the course of the river itself on the far side, between half and three-quarters of a mile from our bank. On a rough patch, adjoining a clump of briers that we had cut down months before, we parked the car. Sheep were scattered along the apron of the bank; below, hoggs were browsing on the washed Cumberland turf. Lines like delicate wrinkles formed patterns among the sand. Gulls were there on their lawful occasions, and oyster catchers, and waders. It was so quiet, we could hear the faint sucking sounds of an estuary half-asleep.

Derwent pointed with his thumb towards mid-sands. 'Let's gaa yon.'

It seemed reasonable. The tide had turned and was about an hour on the flow, but we could stroll dry-shod in our shepherds' boots for at least another half-hour.

Eb settled himself on a hummock. 'Ah'll bide here.' I had a strong suspicion that he would take a nap while we were away. It had been tatie-pot for dinner, a dish he enjoys to the extent of two good helpings.

Derwent and I walked down to the bank. A gull flew off lazily. The sand felt fairly firm, and the runnels we crossed held no more than an inch or two of water. By now the sun was pale primrose, resting on a faint haze that extended down to earth without actually blotting out the distant fells. The scene had a delicacy that even moved Derwent.

He took his pipe from his mouth, spat, pointed eastward with the stem, and said : 'Yon's bonnie.'

We were almost half-way over. More ghostly fells unfolded, a wraithlike half-circle, and we stood and stared for long seconds. Derwent was the first to turn, his voice sharp in the silence.

'Gocks!'

We were looking at mist pouring in, mist that removed the estuary from sight and flowed around us and beyond us without any seeming movement; it might have been exhaled by the bed of the estuary itself.

'We'd better get back.'

'Aye,' said Derwent, setting off without the slightest hesitation as if he knew exactly where to strike the nearest run of bank. I, too, had a similar idea about direction, and it was not until we had walked about a hundred yards that we began to have doubts. Here was a wide runnel across our way, six inches deep, with a pronounced current. I could have sworn we had never crossed it on our way out. I said so, and Derwent agreed.

'Mebbe we've gaan a bit east-like.'

We changed direction, hoping we were heading north. The mist about us gave no help. When we stood still it seemed to stay still with us. As for the runnels, in theory their flow should have been an obvious guide. But this we did know, that many of them ran for several hundred yards and then bent back. Only the main river would give us certainty. Could we reach its course close to the south bank, we should have to swim.

Again we changed direction, and a thin film of water oozed right across our front. Somewhere in the mist a gull was crying. We had a second's glimpse of it as the ceiling of the mist broke high above our heads to reveal primrose light, and then we were hemmed in again.

We crossed another runnel. In the middle of it we were up to our knees. Both of us were racking our brains for a sensible suggestion and could find none, except to shout and hope that Eb might hear us. We paused, yelled together, listened. The sound we heard was the cry of the gull.

'Mebbe we've been mekin' (making) towards wrang bank.'

One guess was as good as another. In quick succession we crossed two channels flowing in opposite directions.

Derwent said: 'A chap might break neck on fells. Aye. But ah niver thought ah might git drooned.' He relit his pipe, glanced about into the masking greyness. 'We're a pair o' April noddies, gittin' lost.

Wheer d'ye think we might be at?'

'Let's go this way,' I said, because it was in front of us, and for no other valid reason. 'We'll keep going, however deep the water.'

We splashed through something more than a runnel, wading up to our waists, came out upon sand protruding from shallows. A note drifted through the mist.

'Harksta!' Derwent raised a hand. 'That's nay a gull.'

It was a whistle, the whistle of a shepherd who could summon his dog at half-a-mile, a whistle produced with two fingers. This time both of us were certain we knew its direction. We splashed and waded on, and the welcome whistling grew nearer. Abruptly, with the trick-photography of the cinema, the bank was before us. Dripping, we trudged up and nearly banged into a standing Eb.

Derwent said: 'Lucky thou can whistle a laal bit.'

Eb's smile was pitying. 'Unlucky thou's got nobbut a laal bit o' sense.'

I laughed. 'Anyway, thanks for bringing us ashore.'

'Aye,' said Derwent. 'Ah'll buy thee hauf a pint.'

'Best mek it a pint. Ah's dry wi' whistlin' at a couple o' gowks.'

It set me wondering about sheep that get cut off by mist. We lose a few on the estuary. Strong swimming and instinct seem to be the salvation of the others that stray into danger.

From the angle of the dalesman, and indeed of Lakeland townsfolk, February is still a very quiet month; the year yet to open its first petals. Strange cars on the roads are rare. There is something about everyday life reminiscent of 20 years ago when petrol rationing and other austerities reigned; when instead of going to the shops the dale wife stayed at home and bought her requirements from the travelling general store and the travelling draper. There was something nicely medieval about this, for it included a full measure of gossip. Up to this very day there exists among the folk of Cumberland, Westmorland and North Lancashire a bond akin to the close relationship of the Highland clans. Now the ubiquitous car carries Mr. and Mrs. Dale-Todd to the nearest town on market day, mostly Thursday. Mr. attends the cattle and sheep sales, and Mrs. enjoys a round of the shops. Likely neither pays much heed to the background. They have known the town since early childhood and familiarity breeds not exactly contempt but a kind of disinterest. That stone building yonder? A fine piece of architecture? Oo, aye, been there a gey long while.

Whitehaven is an example of this sort. Approach it from the south on a fine day and look from the top of the hill that plunges down into the town. Beyond the chimneys of industry and the ancient harbour the Solway glistens across to the Scottish shore. Approach it from the north, and the introduction is totally unexpected, a hill diving between high green banks clustered with old trees. Only when you glance up towards the sky do you find the unashamed challenge of industry. Coal and shipping made Whitehaven; as Liverpool grew, Whitehaven shipping slumped; now coal slumps, and shipping increases, and all day long dredgers are busy on the harbour bar.

The trite saying about beauty being in the eye of the beholder is especially true of Whitehaven. Out of the market once climbed giddy terraces of grimy houses, where a tenant might spit on the roof of the house below; it was locally known as Buggy Bank. The houses have been demolished, and up past this precipitous site a road comes suddenly out. A great chimney shaft is a sentry; a terrace of shaggy grass offers itself as a viewing platform; a cascade of old, cracked, almost sinister stone steps tumbles away to a quay far below. Ahead are the defence bastions that were improved after Paul Jones made his not very effectual raid; they are topped by some semi-ruined, gnarled and yet spell-bound buildings that belong to the art of Arthur Rackham and Heath Robinson; along the skirts of the grim curtain defences, just above the water, yellow wild-flowers and heather have their season. Escaped lumps of coal mark the railway line at the edge of the docks. The old and new lighthouses are toys above the glimmer of the harbour; that wide glitter of blue and silver is the Irish Sea.

Whitehaven specializes in surprises. How many visitors entering the town from the south would dream that within a stone's throw of the road they are descending there runs another, parallel and to the south? I always make a point of pottering there and savouring those period houses. They are delicious, unselfconscious; craning to see their own front gardens laid out on the other side of their own road;

and looking up at Kells, the miners' area, which has its own pride because it occupies the ridge of a tremendous green bank worthy to be called a fell.

The half-castellated building with its park at the east end of Lowther Street was once a town house of Lord Lonsdale. Next it became a hospital and after that a geriatric home. Idling on a seat in the park and enjoying a glint of surprisingly warm February sun, I had as my neighbour a chatty veteran in a wheeled chair. The nurse in charge left him there for a while to fetch another octogenarian. He said: 'Gey fine day,' and I agreed with him. We went on talking for a space. Presently he asked, with a nod of his head towards the building: 'Thou'll be yonder, too, eh?'

It came as such a shock to my ego, all I could answer feebly was: 'Not yet.'

Beyond the wooded steepness at the back of the park is another surprise, a terrace path crossing a grassy slope. It surveys the town, the Solway, the Scottish shore, the Irish Sea, and sometimes the Mountains of Mourne. As a banquet of seeing, this sounds sumptuous. But Whitehaven being unemotional and—if I dare say so—almost unwilling to admit to any charms, the view is taken for granted. Sauntering along the terrace on an afternoon of north-west wind, fleeting black clouds and scuddings of rain, and intervals of such scrubbed and burnished sunshine, far distance became a sharp nearness, I was approached by an old pensioner.

'How d'ye do?' he said.

I smiled and nodded, and he stopped and stuck out his right hand towards the west.

'What's yon?'

He was pointing at the Mountains of Mourne, an imposing dark blue hump beyond the paler silhouette of the Isle of Man.

I told the pensioner. 'Oo, aye,' he said, with supreme unconcern. 'Ah's known this spot fur 70 years. Nivver seen yon before. A laal bit queer, eh?'

In their time the Lowthers must have made a fortune out of Whitehaven and the Harbour. But they brought another fortune to the town itself. Their blue-blooded neighbours, the Curwens of Workington and the Senhouses of Maryport did their intelligent utmost to copy them. Workington prospered with its coal trade, though it never rivalled Whitehaven. The family lineage of the Curwens stretched so far back into antiquity, they must have felt it rather vulgar to bother about money. With Earl Gospatric of Northumberland as their direct ancestor, they looked upon William the Conqueror as a *parvenu* trying to keep up with the Joneses; presumably they hugged the thought to themselves, or they would have lost their lands.

Theirs was the sad privilege of acting as hosts to the exiled Mary, Queen of Scots. Often, glancing at the Solway, I picture that lovely young woman with her heart-shaped face and regal manner standing on the deck of a tiny ship, her back to her lost kingdom, her eyes turned anxiously to the Cumberland shore. After her defeat at Langside on May 13th, an ominous date to the superstitious, she and her few attendants had ridden desperately for the coast, scarcely better off than beggars. Her reception on the English coast was courteous and kind. Sir Henry Curwen and his son met her, and the refugees were escorted with honour to Workington Hall. Such was the condition of Mary and her maids, Lady Curwen provided them with fresh clothes.

In the evening Mary wrote a letter, in French, seeking affection and help of Queen Elizabeth. Sir Henry undertook to have it delivered; having little else with which to express her thanks, Mary gave him a simple Scottish quaigh.

The next morning, May 17th, 1568, was sunny and serene. Under Sir Henry's guidance they started off for Cockermouth, following the course of the Derwent. Ahead, the distant fells were green and inviting, dappled by infrequent cloud shadow. Perhaps Mary looked around with longing, saying good-bye to the tall slopes of Criffel rising from her own forbidden realm.

At Cockermouth she was passed into the care of Henry Fletcher, a wealthy merchant, who lodged her and hers at his house, Cockermouth Hall, and pitying the deplorable state of her wardrobe, gave her thirteen ells of rich crimson velvet. When James I succeeded to the English throne and crossed the border, Henry Fletcher's son,

Thomas, met him at Carlisle, and was knighted for his father's kindness to the king's mother.

At Cockermouth the Percies, the Dacres, the Howards and other great families came to pay Mary homage. She must have been very beautiful at 25, with her lustrous chestnut hair and her new crimson gown; hers was the kind of beauty that earned from men, and from many women, forgiveness for her strange, dark fatal love affairs; but for her beauty, even Elizabeth might have forgiven her.

Nineteen years later, on her last dread day, she wore black in which to die; complexion creams softened her ageing face; an auburn wig hid her grey hair; whatever her thoughts, she was calm, gracious, so that her executioners nearly wept. As the axe ended her life, the wig fell to the floor, and her little pet dog, moaning, leapt upon the headless shoulders. Elizabeth's savage jealousy was appeased at last, and her own end was to be worse than Mary's, dying almost alone, racked in body and tortured in soul by hopeless remorse.

These days Workington Hall is a partial ruin on the higher fringe of the town. It had a ghost that specialized in tidiness and took care of the library. If a book were removed, and put back in the wrong place at eventide, by the following morning it would be in the right place. An elderly acquaintance told me that he was once sitting in the library with his Curwen host and a couple of sleeping hounds; suddenly he became aware that the hounds were awake and bristling, staring at the far door. Growling, their heads turning slowly, they watched an invisible somebody crossing the library to the other door. Then their growling ceased, their hackles went flat, and they resumed sleep.

Were I a dictator, I would restore Workington Hall. Another place I would preserve is that bluff of ancient buildings adjoining Church Street, if only for the sake of visiting Americans who might claim that their own country could offer greater depths of lake and heights of mountain than the Lake District, but would have to hang their heads in silence if I said: 'And what about old buildings? Have you any to compare with these?'

Where Mary rode from Workington to Cockermouth is now a derelict railway. The last time I travelled on it, one or two got on here and there, and one or two got off; between any pair of stations there were never more than seven travellers. I doubt if Cockermouth worried over the closing of the line. Of the smaller towns, probably it has the most intimate connection with fell-dale life. You can feel it and hear it in the main street; the voices of country folk mingle with the noises of cars and buses, and from the auction market not so far away drifts the lowing of beasts. Wordsworth pattered here in infancy, and the house where he was born is solid and attractive evidence that his parents could afford a family. At the opposite end of the town is another distinguished building, Cockermouth Castle, partly used as the estate offices of the Leconfield family.

CHAPTER THIRTEEN

March

March has the trick of being all things to all men—especially in the dales with their mouths opening wide to the Solway. Stroll on the yellow shores and look westward. The breeze is fresh, a frolic yielding promise of spring. I recall standing on a slope above Crosscanonby, north of Maryport, the morning bright in early March and gazing over to Galloway, where the cloud shadows and the dimples of sunshine chased inconsequently. I felt I was watching a teasing June on a stretch of coast that had changed not at all in a thousand years. Then I turned about, and glowered at winter.

Generally, if a sou-wester is blowing, the salt of it can be tasted on the back of one's hand, as far as the barriers of the western fells. Cross the tops of them to the inner valleys, and the salt is gone and the air has harshness. Even so, there are exceptions among exceptions. Here and there, within the orbit of the western warmth, crouch farmhouses tightly tucked against steep fell-breasts that face north. Some catch no sunlight in winter for a full 12 weeks, drowned in the sepia shadow of the fell. The ground about them stays hard and cold. A farm a half-mile distant may be blazoned with brilliance. Lucky the folk and the sheep and the grazing facing south.

The inner valleys, too, have their thrice-welcome exceptions, sanctuaries in the shape of shielded hollows. Daffodils gleam in the bowl of Broughton Mills at the same time as snowdrops are shuddering a mile or two away. Ice glitters on shaded crags, snow dwells white and hard and shiversome in the clutch of gullies, cornices curve out from the eastern ribs of the Scafells—and a little way off there is peeping greenery, perhaps wood sorrel on the banks of the Esk. The foot accustomed to pavements will meet amusing surprises. Some thawed track or trod, raised by frost, drops and quivers under the weight of the walker as if the way were resting on delicate wire springs. There is the occasional breast of soil, a new green plumpness, buoyed up by unseen water below it. Step upon this, and the sensation is like treading upon a half-inflated tyre.

The ravens pay no heed to the fickle variations of local weather. They nest early, before the rest of Nature has finished yawning, and care nothing for petty enemies like ice or snow. Strong, dark, sardonic, they have increased during the last 20 years, untroubled by chemical fertilizers and the side-effects of weed-killing sprays and the dripping of baneful sheep-dips. I recommend the human visitor in March to watch for those powerful black-feathered bodies cruising on their cloudy ventures, or diving in a sudden victory-roll. That cry of 'pronk, pronk' has an apt note of the sepulchral on a grey, silent, lonely day. But I care to believe that the raven is not so forbidding as he pretends. Observe him anywhere, over Scafell or the Pike, Coniston Old Man, Skiddaw, Helvellyn, the lesser fells, parading with his mates, delving into the remains of a dead yow, launching an attack at a passing buzzard. He gives the impression of enjoying life.

Another creature often busy at this time, and easy to see, is the ermine. I prefer the old rich name, rather than calling it a winter stoat. We had one here that haunted our precincts for months, a most exclusive and elegant specimen. Many of his kind are merely white smeared with brown or brown smeared with white, but this Beau Brummel was all pure whiteness except the black tuft at the tip of the tail. I used to watch him from my bedroom window just after first light. At a distance, gliding and changing direction smoothly, he resembled a tiny pale gull skimming a few inches above the winter grasses. Somehow I had the conviction that he was lolloping around for the pure joy of it, and not for any carnal purpose such as hunting his breakfast. I would stand with my tie half-knotted, my nose against the chilly glass, admiring the ripple and the grace of him.

These quiet months, quiet in the sense of absence of human beings, encourage wild creatures to be less discreet. My best glimpses of the ermine's big cousin, the pine marten, have been in the late autumn and the very early spring. At the turn of this century, according to Will Porter, late Master of the Eskdale and Ennerdale Hunt, hounds killed four or five sweetmarts, as they are known, for every fox. This sounds like regrettable slaughter. Yet there is the other side, the wholesale destruction of poultry, and even of full-grown sheep.

There came a phase when men believed the mart to be extinct. A few pairs survived in the most inaccessible crags. The expansion of forestry helped the marts. Among the trees they were safe from hunting. Nowadays, though not plentiful, they at least hold their own. On a sharp, moonlit midnight I met one along our dale road. It scuttled up the flanking wall, sat on the cam stones, and showed its teeth. Under the moon its rufous brown coat gleamed lustrous. I caught no scent, though old folk claim that it gives off a pleasing perfume, quite different from its smelly relative, the foulmart or polecat.

With the higher fells still frozen, the hardy may enjoy themselves up there, wearing nailed boots and carrying ice-axes. Those less suitably equipped should choose safer enjoyments. St. Bees and St. Bees Head qualify to be within the spell of the Lake District. There is no dishonour in turning the back upon frozen fells to spend half a day wandering through a large pink village and its ancient church, and standing dizzily near the edge of a great pink cliff that plunges down into the Irish Sea.

The village is easy enough to find, and leads the seeker down to where the old school and the old church face each other. This pink sandstone that warms the eye could tell intriguing stories. For 400 years it has served the school, and for 900 the church. True, the stone has flaked, time eroding the carvings about the magnificent Norman doorway; some of the crooked pillars upholding the roof could make a thirsty motorist wonder whether he was fit to drive; for sandstone, like everything else in this world, is vulnerable. It came from quarries that supplied stone to London for Victorian office buildings; more of it helped to erect town-halls in the north of

England; more of it was shipped from Whitehaven to New York. St. Begha, the saintly maiden who fled from Ireland to escape the attentions of a wicked baron, and gave St. Bees its name, must look down from Paradise and smile at the thought of her sanctuary in Cumberland proving so fruitful.

St. Bees Head, less easy to find, is reached by a rough lane branching coastwards from the village of Sandwith. A careful car can be coaxed to the lighthouse. After that there is a walk across an airy field, and a gasp as the land ends in a pink, shattered precipice.

Choose your day, keep a foot or two from the edge, and take your time surveying the Irish Sea and the Solway, Man, the Kingdom of Mourne, and the Galloway coast. Land across the sea always conjures up mystery and invitation. Picture poor little St. Begha, in an open boat with her maiden attendants, drifting towards this great, foreign headland, and wondering what could be in store for her, exiled by the dread of losing her honour. At least the wife of the lord of the land treated her with respect and affection. Presently St. Begha was to implore the great man to grant her enough land to build and endow an abbey. Unlike his pious lady, he had little reverence for Mother Church, and with acid humour offered all the land around that should be covered with snow on Midsummer's day. On the vital morning she awoke to see the countryside blanched for a distance of three miles. The legend has charm, and maybe a savour of truth. After all, I have seen snow on Pillar in June, and in the gullies of Great End in July.

Another story belonging to this huge overhang falling into nothingness is no legend but brave, sad truth. I am unlikely to forget that Saturday afternoon 20-odd years ago. Some members of a local natural history club, deciding that the best way to view the bird life of the cliff would be from the sea, set out in a small boat with an auxiliary motor. There were six of them, four men and two women. The sea was choppy, with a brisk breeze from the west and the tide on the flow. They shipped water, and it put the engine out of action. Hurriedly they ran up a sail. The mast went, and then the tiller broke away. Helpless, they were washed towards the towering buttress of sandstone. One of them pointed out a narrow ledge, just above where the waves were breaking. Could they reach that, it would mean another hour of life, and the ghost of a chance of being saved. They waited, ready to spring and snatch, and then one of the men gave a signal. The boat bumped against the rock. There was a smother of spray. In the confusion, three of the men on the ledge imagined that one of the women had been left in the boat. They jumped down, and the sea claimed them, and therein their honour dwells. Cramped on the ledge, spattered with rising foam, the survivors waited for death.

Two small boys were out that afternoon. From the top of the cliff they saw what had happened, and rushed to the lighthouse. Coastguards, police and firemen, using ropes 300 feet long, rescued the survivors.

To this intimidating cliff belongs a third story, probably untrue, humorous in a macabre fashion, and without any detailed end. Where the sea-birds weave and scream there is a freak of geology, a spur of rock jutting out from the main face, a narrowness ending in a tiny, tilted plaform, a sight to give even a hardened climber a spasm of nausea. The place is known as Lawson's Leap. One of the daredevil Lawsons, a notable Cumberland family, was out hunting. The hard-pressed fox streaked for the edge of the cliff, and leapt clean across to the platform. Lawson spurred his horse and followed suit. There is no explanation of how they brought him and the horse back, nor whether the fox somehow made its escape.

To the right, with heather in attendance, the track follows the line of the cliff towards Whitehaven, and to the left it dips towards Fleswick Bay and its semi-precious stones.

It needs no expert geologist or geographer to notice a strange feature of this coastline. In places the cliffs are very much higher than the land behind. From an inlet flanking Whitehaven runs a narrow valley, almost at sea level, right through to St. Bees. It would not be impossible to imagine a tidal wave bursting into one end and gushing out the other.

I dare not omit Furness Abbey from any account of the Lake District, and since the direct way from St. Bees passes Millom, to miss the Old Church there would be a loss as well. A mile out of the town, and immediately beyond the ruins of Millom Castle, it resembles an antique prayer converted into a stone and timber reality, if I may use a fanciful simile. What it was like before restoration I can only guess, but this I vow; a pagan would acknowledge its atmosphere, its effect of wisdom and peace. Resting on a low knoll, the countryside at its doorstep, it blends the feeling of medieval pomp and power with a curious undertone of modesty, as if some old abbot himself were saying to his monks: 'We are all servants to one another.'

Perhaps this is the mood in which to pay the next homage, to Furness Abbey. Guide books galore describe it in detail. Pamphlets give its history, its measurements. It seems impertinent to say any more about it, apart from running the risk of boring by repetition. And yet I dare to believe that because Furness is out on a limb, and inextricably linked with the shipbuilding reputation of Barrow, large numbers of people know little about it except its name.

Its secretive valley, Beckansgill, the vale of the deadly nightshade, was pierced by the railway a century ago. A road runs within hearing of it. Something nameless and powerful, a kind of benevolent emanation, tames these intrusions. It is lovely, extraordinary, and a fact. The abbey was dedicated to the Blessed Virgin, and came into being as a filiation of the monastery of Savigny in Normandy, belonging to the Benedictines. Despite the Dissolution in 1537, the words of dedication seem to have cast their spell forever.

'In the name of the Blessed Trinity, and in honour of St. Mary of Furness, I, Stephen, Earl of Boulogne and Moreton, consulting God, and providing for the safety of my own soul, the soul of my wife, the Countess Matilda, the soul of my lord and master, Henry, King of England and Duke of Normandy, and for the souls of all the faithful living as well as dead, in the year of Our Lord 1127 of the Roman indiction, the 5th. and 18th. of the epact. Considering everyday the uncertainty of life, that the roses and flowers of kings, emperors and dukes, and the crowns and palms of all the great wither and decay: and that all things, with an uninterrupted course, tend to dissolution and death, I, therefore, return, give, and grant to God and St. Mary of Furness all Furness and Walney . . . with this object and condition: That in Furness an order of regular monks be by divine permission established; which gift and offering I, by supreme authority, appoint to be forever observed, and that it may remain firm and inviolate for ever, I subscribe this charter with my hand, and confirm it with the sign of the Holy Cross.'

Let us remain in unknown Lancashire for the rest of this March day. The Rusland valley will be mild and untroubled, its lanes tendering promise of spring. How many in the south realize that Lancashire's share of the Lake District is a major slice, that the county has the sense of humour of Wigan, that its talk of clogs and shawls, and granite setts and mill chimneys is a good-humoured misleading of the general public? Rusland, Bouth, Satterthwaite, these are names describing places that are hard to describe, since they boast no visual drama. No. They resemble quiet music, the kind that lulls and soothes away all cares. Woods, streams, the hills protecting them, they make no attempt to startle or to impress, but simply induce all that is restful. Curiously, in less scientific days, Rusland had an industry, and a rather wicked one at that. It made gunpowder. The carpets of small timber were used for charcoal, and dotted about among the spinneys were the bothies of the charcoal burners. They were still busy during the 1914-18 war.

Nature has covered the traces of the charcoal-burners. It has patterned the whole valley with a leafage that seems to lend even more silent confusion to its wandering lanes. Suffer no worry if you lose yourself. Drift on happily, forget the time, and emerge eventually somewhere in the neighbourhood of Hawkshead. Locals call it 'Arkseid', which might, I imagine, be bewildering to a foreigner inquiring his way. Among its treasures are the old Grammar School, attended by Wordsworth. Close by, in the Beatrix Potter house at Sawrey, it would be easy to believe that she still dwells there. Nobody with a ghost of imagination would call it a mere museum. It lives and laughs and makes those oft-read stories and their characters come true.

Before the building of the railway, the Abbey and Furness generally were remote, almost unvisited. The barriers of the fells and the estuaries involved the pilgrim in tortuous travel. Until this day the arrogant car has to accept long deviations. The train provides the shortest journey. It was this difficult approach of tall hills and wide water that kept the Lake District unchanged for so long. Local folk used the route across the sands of Morecambe Bay and the Duddon estuary. It was ever-changing, difficult, dangerous. Paid guides checked the shifting sands daily, and marked the changes with clumps of brushwood. The difference in distance between the over-sands and the overland ways was such, folk were tempted to take risks, and the toll of tragedy ran high, including a large party of guests returning from a wedding.

These days there is an occasional organized walk across the bay, conducted by a guide, but the Duddon crossing exists no longer. A motorist who can do without his car for once should sample the trip by train from Askham to Millom, along the great curve of coast-line flanking the Duddon waters. Here are stretches denied to the car. To vary his day, he can then resume driving, and if the March air stings and the high fells loom bleak and wintry, he may cruise among sheltered places. Not far off are the twin privacies of Broughton Mills and Broughton Moor, maybe a month ahead of their still shivering neighbours. Broughton Mills, that kindly tureen of grass and trees, basks between Dunnerdale and the Broughton-Coniston road. The good Lord might have created it especially as a setting for hound-trails. You stand in a meadow and smile at the colour and speed of the hounds flowing around the uplands of the amphitheatre. Here, on a March day, you may be able to idle and purr, while folk a mile or two further on wear red noses and blow their hands.

Broughton Moor is evasive. It plays a game of hide-and-seek, which strikes me as fair enough, since the best things are seldom gained easily. The road to it from Broughton Mills—and from the Duddon, for that matter—is marked on the map, but the 'Open, Sesame', so to speak, does demand an alert eye. Once across the frontier, any-body who hurries deserves sentence of banishment. The walled and wooded narrowness wanders with the inconsequence of a happy child. Steep twists and turns reveal more steep twists and turns. Some-times you can see quite a distance. Often, the future is a screen of greenery. The bridges are toys, but strong ones. Broughton Moor is what I would call a personal place. On the open fell you are a fragment, a speck, a nothing. Here, you belong to every little curve, and it belongs to you. Perhaps Nature designed it for the use of true children. I recall a wise woman telling me that small children would rather watch a mouse crossing the road than stare at tremendous scenery.

The very names have a fairy tale quality. Here flows, or whispers, or chuckles the Appletreeworth Beck. A gateway by the bridge opens upon a meandering track. It winds and saunters towards the ruin of old Appletreeworth farmhouse, reached by a baby wooden bridge. Everything has the right, small size, the right perspective.

Here I will leave you for a space, because there is work to be done at home. March advances, and we must get ready for the early spring campaign. One night in late March a breeze started to murmur across from the south-west, and for several hours tepid rain rustled through the darkness. By first light the thaw was steadily releasing the steely grip of the frost. God willing, the yows would have ideal lambing conditions, for in dampness and warmth birth comes easily, and seldom requires the coaxing, pitying hands of the shepherd. With the thaw, there would be an inevitable crop of wall gaps, the expanding ground subsiding and producing avalanches of stone.

After breakfast Derwent came in with his report. There were seven gaps. We started on the one nearest the farmhouse, a breach about eight feet wide, its ragged edges curved downwards almost to the level of the earth. Whoever last handled this stretch had been a waller of the old school, most carefully fitting in the layer of smaller stones between the two barriers of bigger stuff. The cams now sprawled on the ground were well matched. The 'throughs', those massive chunks placed here and there across the entire width of the wall to bind it with the pressure of their weight, had been expertly chosen.

While we cleared away more lumps to prepare a firm foundation, Derwent reckoned aloud that walling with Westmorland free-stone was a gey sight easier. Flat and handy, it could be set in position without any bother.

Eb, a purist in these matters, sniffed. 'Thou talks laike a feckless bairn.'

His indirect rebuke was that if you lived in a granite country you should be ready to use the material at hand. These Eskdale granite boulders were all shapes and sizes, and mebbe a laal bit difficult to 'sit' at the first attempt. But they have their merits. A chap needed fewer of these sizeable boulders to fill a gap than them narrow flakes of Westmorland ste-un (stone). Aye.

Derwent made a sound like 'Umph', and gave his view that Westmorland walling was more pleasant to the eye. Them houses in spots such as Ambleside and Windermere, for instance, with those flakes in perfect line, and nay evidence of cement between them, being tilted down a laal bit to hide the cement at their inner ends—was there owt as bonnie in granite country? He turned his head and winked at me.

Eb said scathingly: 'Nay, don't talk sae daft. Them places are nobbut young lassies. There's nay body to 'em. Now, granite—.' He jerked his thumb at the portly boulders forming the walls of our barn.

''Tis a matter o' te-aste (taste),' said Derwent.

Eb shook his head, and vowed there were no wallers of any worth among the younger generations.

'If thou'd git aboot a bit mair (more),' said Derwent, 'thou'd see thou was wrang.'

He quoted the county roadmen, and the jobs they had been doing of late. There was Throstlegarth bridge, that age-old humpback at the confluence of the Esk and the Lingcove, weakened and at last brought down by a succession of floods. 'Twas hard to tell the difference between the new bridge and the old, the workmen getting their material from the rocks littering the fells. A long, patient job that, for out of every 100 pieces of granite they picked and tested, 90 had been rotten. There was the new bridge over the Logan Beck on Corney Fell, and—

'Ah's seen it,' said Eb quickly. 'Ste-uns (stones) was cut by machine.'

Derwent said: 'How many folk would notice that?'

'Ah would.'

'Then there are a' them new lay-bys an' passin' spots. Tek t'road from Broughton to Coniston—or oop Grizebeck. That new wallin' is fair lovely.'

'Ste-uns was cut by machine.'

Derwent winked at me again. "'Tis his theme song.' He lifted one end of a 'through', and with Eb supporting the other, it was steered into position, two and a half hundredweight of pinkish-grey granite. In an hour the gap was filled, slightly pale in its newness against the flanking stones. But this north side, at any rate, would soon acquire lichens and mosses and miniature ferns.

Some day, perhaps, an enthusiast will write a book devoted entirely to Northern walls, the various kinds of stone in them, and the various colonies of vegetation that bedeck them. A visitor could well spend a day with an admiring eye and a ready camera. Here are the broad walls sometimes seven feet wide at the base and six at the top. They owe their corpulence to some farmer, creating a new field, having to clear the great clutter of stones from the ground and pile them up on the boundaries. There are the adjuncts of walls; the hogg-hole, a gap in the base, wide enough to take sheep, and easily blocked with a large slab; usually, close to a hogg-hole is the grike for the use of the farmer, a stepping-stone below a slit left in the top of the wall, this latter plainly not catering for a Billie Bunter. An alternative to this is a series of slabs sticking out diagonally, on either side of the wall, and suggesting a double ladder of giant petrified mushrooms.

As to gate stoops, Eb has a warm regard for the natural monolith, some pillar chiselled by nature, six feet or so high. In boyhood he was paid a penny an inch for boring the hole to take the iron shank of the sneck. Derwent, too, approves these monoliths, preferring them to three or four boulders cemented in the shape of a stubby tower. These are plentiful, compared with the slop, which might be likened to a starved tombstone pierced with holes to take wooden bars. One of our gates has a slop fixed to the top of a convenient boulder that must be seven feet tall and weighs tons. The upper pivot of the gate revolves inside the slop.

Now, as the veins of March quicken towards April, an early Easter is upon us. We who are involved in Mountain Rescue wish that the Festival could be fixed, given a date late in April, with the likelihood of safer, more genial weather. After all, this is the first public holiday of the year, and the out-of-doors visitors ache to be on high. March often wreaks swift treachery, and death from exposure on a lost walker. The Church disagrees with us, pointing out that Easter is a Holy celebration, not a sort of extended Bank Holiday.

Our reply would be that their answer would have been right once, but is so no longer. At least, the true Easter significance tends to lose some of its meaning, though in the quiet parts of Lakeland some of the customs linger on pleasantly. Until recently, one of the Easter preludes was the display of Easter eggs, bright with their silver, gold, scarlet, or blue wrappings, in the windows of farmhouses and cottages wherever there were bairns. I often hoped that the sun would not shine too strongly to melt the chocolate.

Pace eggs are still with us, but not so obviously in evidence. Our bairns take the boiling of them seriously. If Easter is late, they use the yellow lilies as a stain. If not, whin blossom is a good substitute. Some prefer green, and crushed ivy leaves, boiled with the eggs, give them the necessary tint.

Around our villages, pace-egging during a fine Easter had the brisk liveliness of a race-meeting. All the bairns and a good many of the grown-ups would be gathered by some convenient grassy spot. Eggs would be rolled at one another in combat, and champions, like eight-ers, ten-ers and so forth in the game of conkers, were hailed with respect.

Eb owned the champion egg of all time, a darkish brown veteran that became famous for miles around. Children begged to be allowed to see it, and looked upon it with the veneration a perfect knight would have shown to the Holy Grail. But nobody was allowed to touch it.

'Nay,' he would say, 'ah daren't tek t'risk. It might git cracked.'

After a host of victories it was put away into honourable retirement. But every Easter the children persuaded him to bring it out for one exhibition contest. It would be pitted against the season's

champion, and voices were hushed and breaths held as the current
champion and the ancient veteran met. Always the veteran won.
Some of the very young, I heard, included the welfare of this
wonderful egg in their prayers.

The children yearned to stroke it, as they might caress a kitten.
But Eb was adamant.

'Nay, thou maunt touch. Aye, 'tis a fair capper. But s'pose thou
bruk it somehow in handlin'?'

The thought set them shuddering. Grown-ups smiled at one another, and guessed the truth, and eventually I tackled him about it.

'Aye,' he said calmly, ''tis wood.'

'You old fraud!'

He chuckled and shook his head. 'What's wrang aboot it? Yon
egg's given laal lasses an' lads sicca lock (such a lot) o' pleasure,
ah's nay gaan to repent.'

On Good Friday I have to take care not to go near Eb's cottage.
Eb's wife still clings to the old custom of making a confection of
figs, to be offered to a guest on Good Friday. Whether green or pre-
served, figs to me are nauseating, perhaps because in childhood I was
doctored with the 'syrup of—' variety. Though Eb and his wife have
a television set, and approve the amenities of science, tradition
governs them with decent firmness. To refuse a fig on Good Friday
is wrong, tantamount to sacrilege. The conviction is based on the
belief that the Cross on which they crucified Christ was made from
the wood of a fig tree.

There is a lot to be done in the last days of the month. Already
yows in lamb are drifting down from the fell of their own accord
and whickering outside the intake gate. Unlike their attitude during
the summer gather for clipping, when they resent losing the freedom
to roam, their mood now is quiet, amenable, as if they realize that
more safety and more food await them below. But even in their
advanced and interesting condition, they can jump with elan. So
Eb and I are off to the dale pastures with lengths of wire and posts.
In places the old wire has rusted, or the posts have rotted away.
We drive in the new ones with a large mallet we call a mell, and
run the wire along about a foot higher than the top of the wall. This

usually baffles the most athletic yow, for at the apex of her leap her black muzzle bumps the wire, and back she drops.

Next, we have to tackle something we should have done earlier, the cutting of the briers. Every year they manage to produce new tentacles, no matter how fierce the winter. They grow and thrive when other vegetation fears to leave the shelter of the earth. Besides dragging tufts of wool out of a victim, they will bind her fast. The caught yow twists and turns, plaiting the briers until they are thick enough and strong enough to moor a barge. Then the job of release requires time, and a strong, sharp knife.

For normal cutting, Eb prefers a sharpened spade. My own choice is the long-handled pair of clippers devised for cutting the horns of rams. Progress seems slow, for briers have a touch of the eel about them, wriggling and slithering clear of the steel edges. Eb employs a kind of diagonal swipe, stylish, but frightening. We hope to remove the worst of the briers in a couple of hours.

Eb lights his pipe and takes a rest. 'Aye,' he says, with no particular reference to anything, 'aye.'

If the habit ever dies out of dale conversation, it will be a loss. There is something strangely reassuring about the repetition of the one word.

With a fork I toss cut briers into a heap. Come a dry spell, they should be ready for burning in a few days. The afternoon is quiet, the naked trees stilly by the river, and the barren fells retain their sterile winter colours, gun-metal, dark blue, grey. Yet somehow the dale has a sentience, the implication that another season of life and growth is stirring in the womb of the year.

Eb grunts, jerks his thumb. He speaks of Ambleside, Windermere, Keswick, an' sich-like. Them gift shops in them spots 'll be stockin' oop fur the visitors. Oo, aye.

He sniffs with a phantom of disparagement.

I venture to point out that we, in our own way, are stocking up, too. Visitors, sheep, and forestry. They are the three forces that keep the Lake District ticking over.

He stares up at the crumpled fells, and nods in a contented way.

'Aye, likely thou's reet.'

Index

The numerals in **bold** type refer to the figure numbers of the illustrations

Index

Index

221

Index

Index

Index